FOUR STUDIES IN WORDSWORTH

PORTRAIT OF WORDSWORTH BY HENRY INMAN

Four Studies in Wordsworth

By
Marian Mead

HASKELL HOUSE
Publishers of Scholarly Books
NEW YORK
1964

First Published 1929

HASKELL HOUSE PUBLISHERS LTD.
Publishers of Scarce Scholarly Books
280 LAFAYETTE STREET
NEW YORK, N. Y. 10012

Library of Congress Catalog Card Number: **65-15890**

Haskell House Catalogue Item # **596**

Printed in the United States of America

AUTHOR'S NOTE

Wordsworth's Eye, now altered in a few details, originally appeared in the *Publications of the Modern Language Association of America* (xxiv, 2).

The edition of Wordsworth's *Guide to the Lakes* referred to throughout, is the admirable one of Professor de Sélincourt, Oxford University Press, 1906.

My thanks are due to several friends for help of various kinds in connexion with this book; also to the Reverend J. Farnworth Anderson, of Leicester, England, for obtaining for me the photographs of the Wordsworth garden.

Messrs. Charles Scribner's Sons have kindly permitted use of their reproductions (in *Scribner's Magazine* for February, 1920) of the portrait of Wordsworth and the sketch of Rydal Mount, both by Henry Inman. This New York artist was sent in 1844 by Henry Reed, of the University of Pennsylvania, to paint the portrait of his friend the poet which now hangs in the library of the University. The likeness was thought by Wordsworth and his family to be the best achieved by any artist—Wordsworth had sat twenty-seven times for his likeness. The portrait's full history, from which the above details are taken, is given by Esther Cloudman Dun in the issue of *Scribner's Magazine* mentioned (p. 251).

The especial interest of this picture is in the eyes. It usefully supplements the Haydon portrait also, by giving a pose of the head in which its ideal build is freshly seen.

The inscription on the stone seen in the plate facing page 84 thus celebrates the cedar planted by Wordsworth and Sir George Beaumont:

The embowering rose, the acacia, and the pine,
Will not unwillingly their place resign;
If but the cedar thrive that near them stands,
Planted by Beaumont's and by Wordsworth's
    hands.
One wooed the silent Art with studious pains:
These groves have heard the Other's pensive
    strains;
Devoted thus, their spirits did unite
By interchange of knowledge and delight.
May Nature kindliest powers sustain the Tree,
And Love protect it from all injury!
And when its potent branches, wide out-thrown,
Darken the brow of this memorial Stone,
Here may some Painter sit in future days,
Some future Poet meditate his lays;
Not mindless of that distant age renowned
When Inspiration hovered o'er this ground,
The haunt of him who sang how spear and shield
In civil conflict met on Bosworth-field;
And of that famous Youth, full soon removed
Form earth, perhaps by Shakespeare's self approved,
Fletcher's associate, Jonson's friend beloved.

                                        1808

CONTENTS

LIST OF ILLUSTRATIONS

Frontispiece—PORTRAIT OF WORDSWORTH BY HENRY INMAN

WORDSWORTH'S EYE

The poetry of Wordsworth seems, at first thought, to draw less from the visual sense than that of Milton, or Shelley, or Keats, or many another.[1] For Wordsworth's manner is not a pictorial manner; his poetic methods are not those of the artist; he was no searcher out of the striking; and beauty, as commonly understood, was not to him the supreme inspiration.

Those who are not of the company of true believers will assent with warmth to these observations; but will not, perhaps, be so ready to admit that other manners, methods, and inspirations may be as truly poetic, as rich in the life-giving power which is the final test of poetry. This power in Wordsworth's is in fact derived in remarkable measure from the faculty of the eye. How peculiarly it is so can be only roughly and partially outlined here; the body of his work is the full testimony. Such a sketch, again, however desirable, could hardly be made at all but for one circumstance, sole encouragement of the rash attempter. This is the immensely important fact that Wordsworth, especially

---

[1] When this paper was written (1918), the importance of the eye in Wordsworth was less fully recognized than now. Professor Garrod's book (*Wordsworth: Lectures and Essays*. Oxford, 1923), so illuminating in many directions, makes it impossible for future students to ignore or underestimate this matter. See his pp. 78-79, also chapter VI, *Eyes and Ears*.

I

in his *Prelude,* letting us, more fully, perhaps, than any other poet, into the secrets of the poetic consciousness, has revealed and opened out to us as no one else, however rich in visual imagery, the peculiar function of the eye.[1]

Critics of the poet have noticed his "eye-mindedness." M. Legouis remarks that "his poems contain practically nothing that did not come to him either through hearing or through sight," and, while not emphasizing the dominance of eye over ear, as does Professor Harper, in his recent *Life of Wordsworth,* he observes that the poet was "entirely wanting in ear for music," was "long unable to distinguish one air from another," and called Coleridge "a perfect epicure of sounds." M. Legouis has also commented on the apparent weakness of another sense: "His flowers have no scent. He did not breathe those 'soul-dissolving odours' so dear to Shelley. Roses are seldom met with in his poetry, their fragrance scarcely once." The truth is, Wordsworth lacked the sense of smell. The *Memoir* of him, written by his nephew, tells us that "With regard to fragrance, Mr. Wordsworth spoke from the testimony of others; he himself had *no sense of smell.* The single instance of his enjoying such a perception, which is recorded of him in Southey's life, was, in fact imaginary. The incident

---

[1] It is not intended here to speak of Wordsworth's interest in such visual perceptions as form, mass, motion, light, and colour, but only to consider his faculty of sight in itself, and the relation in him of physical to poetical or spiritual vision.

occurred at Racedown, where he was walking with Miss H——, who coming suddenly, upon a parterre of sweet flowers, expressed her pleasure at their fragrance—a pleasure which he caught from her lips, and then fancied to be his own." To Southey the poet often expressed his regrets for this privation.[1]

Whether the visible world projected itself more sharply, richly, insistently, upon the eye of Wordsworth than upon that of Dante, Milton, Keats, or Shelley, we cannot know; but from what he tells us we do know that his visual impressions were of a very special intensity, and such come to few beholders on this earth. "The bodily eye" he calls "in every stage of life the most despotic of our senses," and speaks of "these visual orbs" as "inconceivably endowed." He tells what delight of the eye he knew when, a child of ten, he drank in

> a pure
> Organic pleasure from the silver wreaths
> Of curling mist, or from the level plain
> Of waters coloured by impending clouds.

And, when the moon was rising, though a boy, untouched as yet by fancy, or by any association of "peculiar sense of quietness or peace," "yet have I stood," he says,

---

[1] See *Southey's Life and Correspondence,* Vol. 1, Chapter IX, p. 63, quoted by Henry Reed in the American Edition of *The Memoir of Wordsworth.*

> Even while mine eye hath moved o'er many a
>   league
> Of shining water, gathering, as it seemed,
> Through every hair-breadth in that field of light,
> New pleasure like a bee among the flowers.

In youth, in the days when "the sounding cataract haunted" him "like a passion,"

>   the tall rock,
> The mountain, and the deep and gloomy wood,
> Their colours and their forms, were then to me
> An appetite, a feeling and a love,
> That had no need of a remoter charm,
> By thought supplied, nor any interest
> Unborrowed from the eye.

And he speaks of the "aching joys," and "dizzy raptures" of that time. Familiar as are these lines, how many readers, even lovers of them, fully realise what they reveal of organic sensibility, of intensity of function, of a state approaching possession,—a word which the poet himself used for his seeing?

Wordsworth has most fully set forth, in the first book of the *Excursion*, the "power of a peculiar eye," and its spiritual development, in boyhood; a description which, though professedly of the Wanderer, we cannot doubt to be autobiographical, because Wordsworth confessed the Pedlar to be "what I fancied my own character might have become in his circumstances," and because it agrees with the poet's known experience.

4

The foundation of his mind laid in solitary communion with Nature, "not from terror free," while yet a child he had perceived the presence and power of greatness,

> and deep feeling had impressed
> So vividly great objects that they lay
> Upon his mind like substances, whose presence
> Perplexed the bodily sense. He had received
> A precious gift, for, as he grew in years,
> With these impressions would he still compare
> All his remembrances, thoughts, shapes, and
>   forms,
> And, being still unsatisfied with aught
> Of dimmer character, he thence attained
> An active power to fasten images
> Upon his brain, and on their pictured lines
> Intensely brooded, even till they acquired
> The liveliness of dreams. Nor did he fail,
> While yet a child, with a child's eagerness
> Incessantly to turn his ear and eye
> On all things which the moving seasons brought
> To feed such appetite.

This, then, is Wordsworth's own account of the astonishing origin and development of the visualising faculty which was so remarkable in itself and so strikingly characteristic of him. His power of seeing again in memory what had impressed eye and mind, all his readers have met, in its gentler aspect,—that "inward eye, which is the bliss of solitude," "seeing by internal light," reviving with a flash sights of beauty, forbidding past experience to become "as is a landscape to a blind man's eye."

A scene which impressed him would be, we are told,

> As beautiful to thought as it had been
> When present to the bodily sense . . . .

He says that he would have been sad at the shortness of his stay at Yarrow,

> But that I know, where'er I go,
> Thy genuine image, Yarrow!
> Will dwell with me, to heighten joy,
> And cheer my mind in sorrow.

And on seeing the Highland girl and her home, he exclaimed:

> In spots like this it is we prize
> Our memory, feel that she hath eyes . . . .

"This delightful creature" he expected to see all his life, and probably did, for at the end of his seventy-third year he had her still in "most vivid remembrance."

But this power had also its aspect of force and intensity, corresponding to those of the original seeing. He says of a child that a half-hour's roam "through imperial bowers" and pleasure-gardens

> Would leave behind a dance of images
> That shall break in upon his sleep for weeks.

Of those mourning the beloved dead he writes

Deem not . . . . .
    that having ceased to see
With bodily eyes, they are borne down by love
Of what is lost, and perish through regret.
Oh! no, the innocent Sufferer often sees
Too clearly, feels too vividly, and longs
To realize the vision, with intense
And ever-constant yearning: there—there lies
The excess, by which the balance is destroyed.

The scenes and objects Wordsworth saw in child-hood and early youth became, through this vividness of visual memory, a lifelong possession. A strong, healthy boy, he delighted in all the boisterous sports of his comrades; fortunately for the world, the rowing, riding, and skating were done amid the society also of the lakes and mountains. Thus, when the "vulgar joy," as he calls it, wore away,

    The scenes which were a witness of that joy
    Remained in their substantial lineaments
    Depicted on the brain, and to the eye
    Were visible, a daily sight.

In moments of wildest boyish fun

                the visible scene
    Would enter unawares into his mind,
    With all its solemn imagery, its rocks,
    Its woods, and that uncertain heaven, received
    Into the bosom of the steady lake.

Skating at evening, on Esthwaite Water,

When we had given our bodies to the wind,
And all the shadowy banks on either side
Came sweeping through the darkness, spinning
    still
The rapid line of motion, then at once,
Have I, reclining back upon my heels,
Stopped short; yet still the solitary cliffs
Wheeled by me—even as if the earth had rolled
With visible motion her diurnal round!
Behind me did they stretch in solemn train,
Feebler and feebler, and I stood and watched
Till all was tranquil as a dreamless sleep.

We may believe that the young William was not the
only one of that "noisy crew" who experienced something of this visual illusion; but as no other could
have given it such expression, on no other, either, could
it have descended with the force which causes the
poet, perhaps fifteen years later, immediately after
recording it, to burst into one of his great apostrophes
of wonder and awe toward Nature who has so ministered to him. Another famous episode of his childhood
drew its power from a visual impression not strictly,
but almost, an illusion. The peak seen from the
boat taken stealthily by night, that spectacle which
caused his brain "for many days" to work "with a
dim and undetermined sense of unknown modes of
being," so that "huge and mighty forms that do not
live, like living men" "moved slowly through the mind
by day, and were a trouble to [his] dreams,"—this
"spectacle" appeared as he rowed upon the silent lake:

> When, from behind the craggy steep, till then
> The horizon's bound, a huge peak, black and
>   huge,
> As if with voluntary power instinct,
> Upreared its head. I struck, and struck again,
> And growing still in stature, the grim shape
> Towered up between me and the stars, and still,
> For so it seemed, with purpose of its own
> And measured motion like a living thing,
> Strode after me.

Thus, in the earlier pages of the *Prelude*, Words-worth is "sedulous to trace"

> How Nature by extrinsic passion first
> Peopled the mind with forms sublime or fair,
> And made me love them.

His mind became indeed a "mansion for all lovely forms." At Cambridge, he took "pleasure quiet and profound" in the study of geometry, because

> Mighty is the charm
> Of these abstractions to a mind beset
> With images, and haunted by herself.

In the ninth book of the *Prelude* is a long passage describing the busy play of fancies in his brain at this period; such fancies as fill the second poem to the daisy (1802), when

> wilful Fancy, in no hurtful mood
> Engrafted far-fetched shapes on feelings bred
> By pure Imagination.

9

More important than this playfulness of the mind is the habit he describes of bodying forth figures of fancy or romance, with a living force rare even among poets. For

> Scarcely Spenser's self
> Could have more tranquil visions in his youth,
> Or could more bright appearances create
> Of human forms with superhuman powers,
> Than I beheld, loitering on calm clear nights
> Alone, beneath this fairy work of earth—

an ivy-wreathed ash-tree at Cambridge, under which he would stand "foot-bound, up-looking," "beneath a frosty moon." When, at the boy's first going to school, a drowned man was taken from the water of Esthwaite, "a spectre-shape of terror,"

> no soul-debasing fear,
> Young as I was, a child not nine years old,
> Possessed me, for my inner eye had seen
> Such sights before, among the shining streams
> Of faery land, the forest of romance.
> Their spirit hallowed the sad spectacle
> With decoration of ideal grace;
> A dignity, a smoothness, like the works
> Of Grecian art, and purest poesy.

Walking alone on Salisbury Plain, he "saw our dim ancestral Past in vision clear," in "a waking dream, a reverie" of Briton and Druid, so vivid that with "believing eyes" he beheld, all about him, long-bearded teachers with white wands pointing to starry sky and plain below, sweet sounds of music accompanying.

Wordsworth's eye thus created for him a discipline through which he learned to dwell with images of beauty and romance, and experienced the power of art to purify the ugly things of life; a discipline, too, which saved him, by the acquired wealth of that eye, from the sickliness or unreality common to immature poets. For

> 'mid the fervent swarms
> Of these vagaries, with an eye so rich
> As mine was, through the bounty of a grand
> And lovely region, I had forms distinct
> To steady me; each airy thought revolved
> Round a substantial center, which at once
> Incited it to motion, and controlled.

But the original keenness, the strong retentiveness, of physical vision which made these benefits possible, were also the foundation of a fuller vision, which was not of the sense alone. The phase of Wordsworth's development now to be treated shows, from his own contrasting of it with former experience, how closely heart and imagination had been involved with the eye's delight.

Wordsworth's bitter disappointment in the results of the French Revolution, on which his opening manhood had staked its dearest hopes, vitiating all his mind, left an impress upon "imagination and taste," the history of whose impairment and cure forms the subject of the concluding books of this great autobiographical poem. At this period the visual faculty became indeed his tyrant. His imaginative power suffered, he explains, through "presumption"; he was

> even in pleasure pleased
> Unworthily, disliking here, and there
> Liking; by rules of mimic art transferred
> To things above all art;—

but still more (and here comes a hint of the jealous eye) by

> giving way
> To a comparison of scene with scene,
> Bent overmuch on superficial things,
> Pampering myself with meagre novelties
> Of colour and proportion; to the moods
> Of time and season, to the moral power,
> The affections and the spirit of the place,
> Insensible. . . .

What follows this is most interesting and significant:

> Nor only did the love
> Of sitting thus in judgment interrupt
> My deeper feelings, but another cause,
> More subtle and less easily explained,
> That almost seems inherent in the creature,
> A twofold frame of body and of mind.
> I speak in recollection of a time
> When the bodily eye, in every stage of life
> The most despotic of our senses, gained
> Such strength in me as often held my mind
> In absolute dominion.

He suggests that Nature, to thwart this tyranny, studiously employs all the sense to counteract one another—

But leave we this; enough that my delights
(Such as they were) were sought insatiably.
Vivid the transport, vivid though not profound;
I roamed from hill to hill, from rock to rock,
Still craving combinations of new forms,
New pleasure, wider empire for the sight,
Proud of her own enjoyments, and rejoiced
To lay the inner faculties asleep.

And he adds that "as we grow up, such thraldom of the sense seems hard to shun."

If at this point we recall the youth who "like a roe"

bounded o'er the mountains, by the sides
Of the deep rivers, and the lonely streams,
Wherever Nature led: more like a man
Flying from something that he dreads, than one
Who sought the thing he loved,—

we shall at once feel the change and loss. Yet Wordsworth in this very passage declares that the "appetite" which then possessed him for the colours and forms of Nature had no need of thought, or "any interest unborrowed from the eye." But if anything is true of Wordsworth, it is that in youth, as always, his physical vision was, normally, bound up with spiritual powers. In this same passage, indeed, we must feel them, in its rapture and awe. And he exclaims, at another time, "What visionary powers of eye and soul in youth were mine!" In the apparent contradiction of the *Tintern Abbey* passage, then, the poet returned in memory to a phase in which, though thought and feeling were present, they were not distinct to consciousness from the visual impression, which in its ardour and first fine careless rapture, appeared all in all.

That ardour, indeed, is present even in the period of vitiation. The vivid delight, the insatiability of the eye's demand, the despotism of the sense of sight, "proud of her own endowments," all testify to that force in Wordsworth of the visual faculty which it seems clear we do not usually appreciate, since so sympathetic a critic as Professor C. H. Herford refers to this "tyranny of the eye" as "mere observation," which his sister's "exquisite regard for common things . . . helped to transform . . . into imaginative vision."[1]

One more picture of Wordsworth's youthful experience shows him in the character of "the imaginary Scot of the *Excursion*",

> o'erpowered
> By Nature; by the turbulence subdued
> Of his own mind; by mystery and hope,
> And the first virgin passion of a soul
> Communing with the glorious universe.

Failing to find the repose and peace he asked in thought and intellectual abstraction,

> he scanned the laws of light
> Amid the roar of torrents, where they send
> From hollow clefts up to the clearer air
> A cloud of mist that, smitten by the sun,
> Varies its rainbow hues,—

---

[1] *The Age of Wordsworth,* p. 150.

"a true picture," says De Quincey, "of Wordsworth attempting to silence the mighty battery of his impassioned heart"; and attempting it by an effort—vain, as the poet tells us—to divert the stream of power to that master-sense of seeing.

Such is, roughly, the history of Wordsworth's eye as a fine and powerful organ[1]; an organ without whose unusual endowment we should undoubtedly have lost more than anyone can estimate of what is most characteristic in his work. Before passing to another view of the subject, let us call up, as well as may be, the physical appearance of his eyes, so strikingly described by several of the contemporaries who were so happy as to see them.

"It is agreed by all who have described Wordsworth," says M. Legouis, "that the expression of his eyes was rather of the seer than of the artist. Hazlitt tells us that there was a fire in his eyes as if he saw something in objects more than the outward appearance. De Quincey had seen his eyes "after a long day's toil in walking, ...assume an appearance the most solemn and spiritual that it is possible for the human eye to wear. The light that resides in them seems to come from unfathomed depths; in fact, it is

---

[1] Wordsworth suffered much in his later life from inflammation of the eyes, which made writing difficult for him. A course of picture galleries abroad was once observed to relieve this condition, perhaps by diverting his thoughts from the fear of blindness, which oppressed him; or possibly the focal distance for seeing pictures was the one which best suited his eyes. His trouble was a seriously disabling one. See *Dora Wordsworth Her Book*, p. 81 and p. 86, also Wordsworth's note to *Yarrow Revisited*.

more truly entitled to be held 'the light that never was
on land or sea,' a light radiating from some far spiritual
world, than any the most idealising that ever yet a
painter's hand created." Leigh Hunt wrote: "Walter
Scott said that the eyes of Burns were the finest he
ever saw. I cannot say the same of Mr. Wordsworth;
that is, not in the sense of the beautiful, or even of
the profound. But certainly, I never beheld eyes that
looked so inspired or supernatural. They were like
fires half-burning, half-smouldering, with a sort of
acrid fixity of regard, and seated at the further end
of two caverns. One might imagine Ezekiel or Isaiah
to have had such eyes."

Ellis Yarnall wrote to Professor Henry Reed, of
Philadelphia, of his visit to Rydal Mount. At a remark of his, he says, Wordsworth looked up, "and I
noticed a fixing of his eyes as if on some remote object." Again, "As we returned together he walked
very slowly, occasionally stopping when he said anything of importance, and again I noticed that looking
into remote space . . . His eyes, though not glistening, had yet in them the fire which betokened the greatness of his genius. This no painter could represent,
and this it was which gave to his countenance its high
intellectual expression." A note by Henry Reed (in
the *Memoir of Wordsworth*) observes that "one of the
most accomplished of English portrait painters had
remarked . . . that he had observed in every celebrated person, whose features he had copied, from

the Duke of Wellington downward, this looking of the eyes, as it were, into infinity."[1]

Of the nature of the seeing that was done with those eyes one aspect has been shown; we are now to examine another; to look for the relation in Wordsworth of physical to poetic or spiritual vision.

The period of degradation, of the eye's deliberate quest of its own gratification, was transient. For, says the poet,

> I had known
> Too forcibly, too early in my life,
> Visitings of imaginative power
> For this to last; I shook the habit off
> Entirely and forever, and again
> In Nature's presence stood, as now I stand,
> A sensitive being, a creative soul.

He became once more as in early youth, when he rejoiced with the soul of Nature

> before the winds
> And roaring waters, and in lights and shades
> That marched and countermarched about the hills
> In glorious apparition, Powers on whom
> I daily waited, now all eye, and now
> All ear, but never long without the heart
> Employed, and man's unfolding intellect.

---

[1] Carlyle, however, was not enthusiastic on the subject: "the eyes were not brilliant, but they had a quiet clearness." And Lady Jane Shelley was worse: "Wordsworth, she declared, was hideous," with "small eyes, fireless, and closed with heavy eyelids." "Then she was a young girl, and a young girl is not kind," says Stopford Brooke. Sometimes she is even not discerning. (See *Life and Letters of Stopford Brooke, II,* p. 506.)

This is the true note of Wordsworth's youthful vision;
a note which sounds again when he cries

> Ye Presences of Nature in the sky,
> And on the earth! Ye Visions of the hills!
> And Souls of lonely places! can I think
> A vulgar hope was yours when you employed
> Such ministry, when ye, through many a year
> Haunting me thus among my boyish sports,
> On caves and trees, upon the woods and hills,
> Impressed upon all forms, the characters
> Of danger or desire; and thus did make
> The surface of the universal earth,
> With triumph and delight, with hope and fear,
> Work like a sea?

Through vision, again, he passed at times into a still
deeper region of experience, transcending this perfect
balance of heart and eye, and remote by the full circle's
breadth from the state where the power of the eye
"laid the inner faculties asleep," a region where the
eye's eager delight was subdued by a mightier passion, where sense was lost in spirit.

> For the growing Youth,
> What soul was his, when, from the naked top
> Of some bold headland, he beheld the sun
> Rise up, and bathe the world in light! He
> looked—
> Ocean and earth, the solid frame of earth,
> And ocean's liquid mass, in gladness lay
> Beneath him: Far and wide the clouds were
> touched,

18

And in their silent faces could he read
Unutterable love.   Sound needed none,
Nor any voice of joy; his spirit drank
The spectacle; sensation, soul, and form,
All melted into him; they swallowed up
His animal being; in them did he live;
And by them did he live; they were his life.
In such access of mind, in such high hour
Of visitation from the living God,
Thought was not; in enjoyment it expired.

Wordsworth's seeing thus has, besides the morbid, transient phase of deliberate and exclusive pleasing of the eye, three normal "manners"; a passionate absorption in forms and colours which leaves no room for conscious thought; the equipoise of eye's delight with full activity of both thought and feeling; and the attainment, through sense-perception, immediate or remembered, to an impassioned contemplation where conscious thought again disappears, lost in the deepening tide of joy or wonder.

The great visionary hours of the third manner are not always of the same character.   They may be hours of stillness, reached through a calm and gradual process,—

    that serene and blessed mood,
In which the affections gently lead us on,
Until, the breath of this corporeal frame
And even the motion of our human blood
Almost suspended, we are laid asleep
In body, and become a living soul.

Thus it was when, as a boy, he would go often at dawn, to sit, he says,

> among the woods
> Alone upon some jutting eminence,
> At the first gleam of dawn-light, when the Vale,
> Yet slumbering, lay in utter solitude.
> How shall I seek the origin? where find
> Faith in the marvellous things which then I felt?
> Oft in these moments such a holy calm
> Would overspread my soul, that bodily eyes
> Were utterly forgotten, and what I saw
> Appeared like something in myself, a dream,
> A prospect in the mind.[1]

When he tells of roaming, at Cambridge, "among men and shops," "delighted with the motley spectacle," though in a "loose and careless mood," there is still, in the line

> I was the Dreamer, they the Dream,

a trace of this same visionary state.

But not always in this sort was his existence *"possessed,"* to use his own emphasised phrase. "Gleams of soul-illumination" would descend upon him with an overwhelming suddenness which he likens to a "flash." "I felt," he says,

---

[1] Sir Walter Raleigh (*Wordsworth,* pp. 66-7) says in connection with the above passage, "It was a kind of possession through the eye that became the type of poetic inspiration to him, a possession nowhere better described than in" the lines in question. The whole paragraph from which this sentence is taken bears upon the subject.

Gleams like the flashing of a shield :—the earth
And common face of Nature spake to me
Rememberable things.

The glory and greatness of the human spirit are made
known to him in moments of almost paralysing force
of onrush,
> when the light of sense
> Goes out, but with a flash that has revealed
> The invisible word.

Wordsworth's visualising power, we have seen, built
up in his brain a world of images, the storehouse of
his poetry, the solace of his mind. What we have now
to observe is, that his eye was not only passive and
receptive, but creative. His habit, already described,
of "bodying forth" images of fancy and romance, so
vividly that they seemed actually present to the bodily
eye, discovers a relation of eye and mind in creative
activity. And this relation, of imagination bodying
forth the forms of things unknown, the giving of outward life, more or less real, to inward conceptions,
would appear to be the more usual path of creative
power in poets. Wordsworth's characteristic path was
different, it may be said, opposite; for in his most
distinctive thinking, as well as in the work which most
truly expresses him, what he created entered his mind
from without, commonly through the eye. That is, in
his "mighty world of eye and ear,—both what they
half create, and what perceive," creation grows from

perception; it is no extraneous invention, but actually, in the last analysis, an enlarged, illumined, perception, bringing out forms or meanings which, though to the ordinary observer invisible, are all the time really there. "A plastic power abode with me," he says; sometimes "rebellious," "a local spirit of his own," but in general "strictly subservient" to the course of the actual external world with which it communed.

Consciously creating, he was conscious, also, that what he created was part of Nature, that the mind's creative power is akin to hers:

> I felt that the array
> Of act and circumstance and visible form,
> Is mainly to the pleasure of the mind
> What passion makes them; that meanwhile the
> forms
> Of Nature have a passion in themselves,
> That intermingles with those works of man
> To which she summons him.

The poet's field is "wherever Nature leads"; he, as seer and discoverer, is her co-worker—

> Nature for all conditions wants not power
> To consecrate, if we have eyes to see,
> The outside of her creatures, and to breathe
> Grandeur upon the very humblest face
> Of human life.

Through such seeing does the poet become a creative power,—"the humblest of this band"

Have each his own peculiar faculty,
Heaven's gift, a sense that fits him to perceive
Objects unseen before . . . .
An insight that in some sort he possesses,
A privilege whereby a work of his,
Proceeding from a source of untaught things,
Creative and enduring, may become
A power like one of Nature's.

And of himself, thus "standing by Nature's side," he says,

an auxiliar light
Came from my mind, which on the setting sun
Bestowed new splendour; the melodious birds,
The fluttering breezes, fountains that run on
Murmuring so sweetly in themselves, obeyed
A like dominion, and the midnight storm
Grew darker in the presence of my eye.

The creative faculty in Wordsworth was deeply rooted in the perception of what he calls "analogies,"— relations between the life of Nature and the life of the mind. With his worst pedestrian amble, he conducts us into acquaintance with a habit highly poetic in itself, and most important to be understood:—

I still had loved
The exercise and produce of a toil,
Than analytic industry to me
More pleasing, and whose character I deem
Is more poetic, as resembling more
Creative agency. The song would speak
Of that interminable building reared

By observation of affinities
In objects where no brotherhood exists
To passive minds.

At the age of seventeen,

whether from this habit rooted now
So deeply in my mind, or from excess
In the great social principle of life
Coercing all things into sympathy,
To unorganic natures were transferred
My own enjoyments; or the power of truth
Coming in revelation, did converse
With things that really are; I, at this time,
Saw blessings spread around me like a sea.

And he goes on to say that he had received so much
from Nature that he was content only

when with bliss ineffable
I felt the sentiment of Being spread
O'er all that moves, and all that seemeth still;
O'er all that, lost beyond the reach of thought
And human knowledge, to a human eye
Invisible, yet liveth to the heart;
O'er all that leaps and runs, and shouts and sings,
Or beats the gladsome air. . . . .

At Cambridge, where he sought and won little of the
glory reserved for students of the accepted branches of
knowledge, he continued his own pursuit of wisdom:

I was mounting now
To such community with highest truth—
A track pursuing, not untrod before,
By strict analogies by thought supplied

Or consciousnesses not to be subdued,
To every natural form, rock, fruits, or flower,
Even the loose stones that cover the highway,
I gave a moral life; I saw them feel,
Or linked them to some feeling: the great mass
Lay bedded in a quickening soul, and all
That I beheld respired with inward meaning. . . .
I had a world about me—'twas my own;
I made it, for it only lived to me,
And to the God who sees into the heart.

Here was the fuller and more conscious development
of the power which in boyhood had enabled him to
read in the silent faces of the clouds "unutterable
love"; which had grown in him while

          many an hour in caves forlorn,
And 'mid the hollow depths of naked crags
He sate, and even in their fixed lineaments,
Or from the power of a peculiar eye,
Or by creative feeling overborne,
Or by predominance of thought oppressed,
Even in their fixed and steady lineaments
He traced an ebbing and a flowing mind,
Expression ever varying!

These sympathies worked so strongly in him that
when, though rarely, they were betrayed by outward
looks and gestures, "some called it madness!" And
so it was, he continues,

If prophecy be madness; if things viewed
By poets in old times, and higher up
By the first men, earth's first inhabitants

25

May in these tutored days no more be seen
With undisordered sight.

But what he saw in such moods was neither the fig-
ment of a fervid brain, nor a vague fantasy; but
something really there to be seen, though invisible to
others; something clearly apprehended through the
bodily eye, busy with definite forms,—"lines of difference," as he says;

It was no madness, for my bodily eye
Amid my strongest workings evermore
Was searching out the lines of difference
As they lie hid in all external forms,
Near or remote, minute or vast; an eye
Which from a tree, a stone, a withered leaf,
To the broad ocean and the azure heavens
Spangled with kindred multitudes of stars,
Could find no surface where its power might
    sleep;
Which spake perpetual logic to my soul,
And by an unrelenting agency
Did bind my feelings even as in a chain.

Thus does Wordsworth himself link his eye, "so
richly endowed," with his peculiar creative power, and
unmistakably explain the relation between his physical
sight and the vision of his soul. And he cries, shaken
by a sense of the fateful character of such vision,

O Heaven! how awful is the might of souls
And what they do within themselves while yet
The yoke of earth is new to them!

How strong was the power that so moved him is betrayed in a sonnet written in a light and graceful vein,—

> How sweet it is, when mother Fancy rocks
> The wayward brain, to saunter in a wood,

where when amid green arbours, and "wild rose tip-toe upon hawthorn stocks" the divine urgency comes upon him with the force even of terror:—

> thoughts link by link
> Enter through ears and eyesight with such gleam
> Of all things, that at last in fear I shrink,
> And leap at once from the delicious stream.

The true mystics, we are told, see always in a vivid clearness of detail the sights revealed to them. "A spirit and a vision are not," says Blake, "as the modern philosopher supposes, a cloudy vapour or a nothing; they are organised and minutely articulated beyond all that the mortal and perishing nature can produce. He who does not imagine in stronger and better lineaments, and in stronger and better light, than his perishing mortal eye can see, does not imagine at all." But such vision has not usually, it would seem, so intimate a connection with the activity of the eye as in Wordsworth. The visions, for instance, which Dante so minutely describes in the *Vita Nuova*, in all their sharp particularity of colour, outline, and gesture, came to him sometimes when his eyes were closed in sleep, and always, apparently, without immediate external stimulus. But Wordsworth's visionary state usually depends on, and directly arises from, something objective, perceived at times by the ear, but far more often by the eye.

His characteristic visionary power, thus, lies not in the seeing of "supernatural" forms, but in the discovery of natural ones, of an inward and vital spirit, hidden from passive eyes. His Druids, and his Spenserian forms with more than human powers, however vivid, were no such realities to him as the thoughts lying too deep for tears which the meanest flower could give; as the glorified figure of the mountain shepherd, a giant in the fog, or "flashing" forth under a sudden radiance of sunset; or as those "great allies" of the betrayed patriot, powers that shall work for him in earth, and air, and skies, and even in the common wind, whose least breathing shall not forget him.

In Wordsworth's "analogies," "an unrelenting agency," a consciousness "not to be subdued," linked for him material forms with a moral life, an inward meaning, and showed him "the surface of the universal earth with triumph and delight, with hope and fear, working like a sea." Further possessed, he experienced bewilderment and perplexity, troublings of the spirit, passing into awe,—

> those obstinate questionings
> Of sense and outward things,
> Fallings from us, vanishings;

> Blank misgivings of a Creature
> Moving about in worlds not realized. . . .

Kindled into perhaps a fuller mystic communion (not
to imply that this mood either followed in time or
surpassed in importance the troubled one, which is
especially characteristic of Wordsworth, and lights
up for us more of his individual quality) he beheld
in man and Nature the original realities, the "ideas"
of which material forms are but the passing shows.
He "did converse with things that really are." The
forms of earth became a transparent veil for the mys-
teries they obscure. Then it is, he says, that, asleep in
body, and become a living soul,

> with an eye made quiet by the power
> Of harmony, and the deep power of joy,
> We see into the life of things.

To see into the life of things! this is indeed the
power of Wordsworth. And it is so notwithstanding
that he saw, sometimes, more than he was always able
fully to convey. For "he attributed," says M. Legouis,
"to certain expressions or incidents more emotion than
other people could reasonably associate with them."
And Sir Walter Raleigh remarks that "to the end of
his days Wordsworth, remembering the exuberance of
his own delight in the composition of it, was unable
to convince how the *Idiot Boy* should fail to arouse
the same feeling in every reader." He returns, in

such poems as this and *Peter Bell,* from little-visited regions of the mind, babbling like an inarticulate child of wonders which he seems to himself to be richly describing; his auditors, puzzled, however, too seldom gather from his broken inadequate phrases anything but food for mirth.

But when, in his great hours, insight and expression are at one, we are caught up, in our own measure, into the vision of him who saw, in rocks and trees, and even the loose stones of the road, life, seeing them linked in the universal chain, bedded in a quickening soul; who in ordinary unnoticed acts of men, or happenings of Nature, lighted by some mysterious flash, or shining through glorified air as harvest of the quiet eye, saw the primal, poetic truth which is indeed of all things their life.

The "Poets' Alley" at Cole Orton Hall

The stone closing the vista has an inscription by Wordsworth. (Not in the Wordsworth Garden)

LIGHT AND COLOUR IN WORDSWORTH

Wordsworth's perceptions of light and colour have a special interest, because the great mass of his poetry is so largely the record of what he *saw*. How was he, whose eye was by nature dominant and insatiate, affected by those simplest appeals to it which all of us experience? A study of his sensibility to them, his loves and likings in them, may add a little that is fresh to our comprehension of him.

It is not easy, however, to disengage from his work the treatment of light and colour. One fears to brush the dust from off its wings; and then there are difficulties of classification. The most convenient plan is, first, to observe Wordsworth's use of light and colour in writing of various "goings-on of the universe," as the changes of day and night, and those appearances of skies, water and earth which are most to the purpose; and second, to look more closely into his particular uses of colour, and of light, with its complement, shade. These divisions, however, cannot be made perfectly distinct, and some overlappings and repetition have been unavoidable. For illustrations the *Guide to the Lakes* has been freely used, because, though not verse, it is of the stuff of poetry and invaluable as an expression of Wordsworth's tastes.

FOUR STUDIES IN WORDSWORTH

I

> There is a radiant though a short-lived flame
> That burns for Poets in the dawning east;
> And oft my soul hath kindled at the same,

it is written in one of those laboured Odes in which we look with least reward for the real Wordsworth. But of such kindling of his soul, some of his most characteristic and memorable passages are proof. He tells in the *Prelude* and the *Excursion* of the exaltation and "beatitude" his spirit knew in the solitary hours when, as boy or youth, he beheld the sun "rise-up and bathe the world in light;" how in such moments the measure of his soul

> was filled with bliss,
> And holiest love; as earth, sea, air with light
> With pomp, with glory, with magnificence!

and how, when far and wide the clouds were touched,

> in their silent faces could he read
> Unutterable love . . .

In the early *Descriptive Sketches* he says that if earth had a spot of holy ground, a refuge from distress and place of solitude preparing for heaven, it would be

> Where falls the purple morning, far and wide,
> In flakes of light upon the mountainside.

Thus these dawn-vigils were some of Wordsworth's great creative and spirit-building hours. The sonnet on

Westminster Bridge was the fruit of such an hour. Through a few supreme words, it radiates the very light of opening day—the city, wearing like a garment the beauty of the morning; silent, bare, open to fields and sky; all brilliant and glittering in the smokeless air; never did sun more beautifully steep in his first splendour, valley, rock or hill. The sonnet, like the phrases quoted above, is bathed in a clear and spacious light, a calm breadth which we shall see is characteristic of Wordsworth's treatment of the light of day. The same large light illumines the opening of *Resolution and Independence,* where, after the night of storm, the sun is rising calm and bright; all things that love the sun are out of doors; the sky rejoices in the morning's birth; the grass is bright with raindrops. The sunny calm of this dawn is present to consciousness through all the early part of the poem; it pervades the air filled with the pleasant noise of waters; it broods beyond the calls and cries of birds, it rushes out to view in the racing of the mirthful hare, raising with her feet the mist that glitters in the sun, and is not absent, surely, from that "pool bare to the eye of heaven" where *was*[1] the old man, motionless as a cloud.

These examples show what dawn in its solitude was to him; dawn and its light, so large, so still, daily, for lonely land or sleeping city, revealing afresh their rela-

---

[1] See, as to this emphatic *was,* the *Prose Works of William Wordsworth,* Vol. II, p. 207, ed. Grosart, Moxon, 1816.

tion to the boundless universe, which other hours may forget.

Wordsworth had also a deep interest in the return of the sun to human life and activity. This is well shown by two passages from the *Prelude*, containing the same light-effect, and both dealing with mountain-dwellers— first the Alpine peasant, contented

> from the moment that the dawn
> (Ah, surely not without attendant gleams
> Of soul-illumination) calls him forth
> To industry, by glistenings flung on rocks,
> Whose evening shadows lead him to repose,—

and second, humble Dalesfolk,—how little, he cries, and yet how great!

> For all things serve them: them the morning light
> Loves, as it glistens on the silent rocks.

In *Guilt and Sorrow*, we read, came the dawn,

> opening the silvery east
> With rays of promise north and southward sent,
> And soon with crimson fire kindled the firma-
> ment;

then on the unhappy woman's brow the sight "like dawn of gladness threw, while to her cheek seemed to return its youthful hue."

There are many details of a June dawn in the fourth canto of the *Waggoner*, a poem rich in light and colour

of skies and of mountain mists.   Skiddaw-top "with
rosy light is touched"; we look forth

> o'er wood and lawn
> Hoar with the frost-like dews of dawn

to ruined towers

> Lurking in a double shade
> By trees and lingering twilight made,

and to a multitude of hills,

> Crags, woodlands, waterfalls, and rills,
> Which soon the morning shall enfold,
> From east to west, in ample vest
> Of massy gloom and radiance bold.

Low-hanging mists begin to rise and spread;

> Their skirts of grey
> Are smitten by a silvery ray.

Wordsworth says, we have seen, that it is a "short-
lived flame" that burns in the dawning east; and its inspiration clearly failed him at times, permitting him to
lay upon the innocent brightness of a new-born day a
dull and heavy hand with which he never crushed the
sweetness of the evening.   He was capable of writing

> bright and red
> Uprose the morning sun,

a phrase which has about it a brisk and horrid cheer-fulness.   This feeling of cheerfulness rather beset Wordsworth in his treatment of dawn and day; it is one which requires a little more drapery than he usually gave it to rank as truly poetic.   For instance,

> How cheerful at sunrise the hill where I stood!

and

> The sun above the pine-trees showed a bright and
>   cheerful face—

these lines and, again, two others:

> Sound, healthy children of the God of Heaven
> Are cheerful as the rising sun in May,

are things which lovers of Wordsworth must some-times—not always—wish to pass with averted eye. But

>   vernal mornings opening bright
> With views of undefined delight

may give them courage, increased by remembrance of that spot in the Vale of Langdale

> To the still influx of the morning light
> Open, and day's pure cheerfulness, but veiled
> From human observation,

or of the Scottish burial-ground, with its depressed graves,

> Level with earth among the hillocks green,
> Union not sad, when sunny daybreak smites
> The spangled turf, and neighbouring thickets ring
> With "jubilate" from the choirs of spring!

And full confidence begins to return at

> hark! the birds salute
> The cheerful dawn, brightening for me the east,

and the lines of the *Phantom of Delight*—

> all things else about her drawn
> From Maytime and the cheerful dawn.

A concluding picture of the morning sky must be given, for its beauty, from a letter to Coleridge written in 1799—

> It was a beautiful morning, with driving
> snow showers, which disappeared by fits, and
> unveiled the east, which was all one delicious
> pale orange colour . . . We were tempted to
> look back perpetually on the stream, which
> reflected the orange lights of the morning
> among the gloomy rocks, with a brightness
> varying with the agitation of the current.

(This was near Askrigg.   The whole letter is most ineresting.)

The sun Wordsworth calls

Divinest object which the uplifted eye
Of mortal man is suffered to behold.

It is the source inexhaustible of life and joy, and "type of man's far-darting reason." He associates it almost invariably with feelings of joy, usually of a very simple nature. "The sun's glad ray," "the heart-cheering sun," "clear shines the glorious sun above"—these are some of his more ordinary expressions of the feeling which at its best fills the fourth stanza of the *Immortality Ode* with the light and joy of the sweet May morning,—

while the sun shines warm,
And the babe leaps up on his mother's arm.

The sun "showers upon the unsubstantial brotherhood of clouds visions with all but beatific light enriched." After storm, "the sun broke out in power, and gladdened all things." It gilds with ready sunbeams every passing shower, and it is Joy

Who with a sunbeam for his guide,
Smoothly skims the meadows wide.

The Solitary of the *Excursion*, wandering with his young bride, says that they saw

The shining giver of the day diffuse
His brightness o'er a tract of sea and land
Gay as our spirits, free as our desires;
As our enjoyments, boundless.

The sun here is associated not only with the feeling of gaiety, but with the idea of freedom and infinitude. To the freedom is added, in another passage, the loneliness of the sun: primitive man is

> Free as the sun, and lonely as the sun,
> Pouring above his head its radiance down
> Upon a living and rejoicing world.

It was through the influence of "many a thoughtless hour of a child's overflowing happiness" that Wordsworth "began to love the sun";—

> a boy I loved the sun,
> Not as I since have loved him, as a pledge
> And surety of our earthly life . . .
> But for this cause, that I had seen him lay
> His beauty on the morning hills, had seen
> The western mountain touch his setting orb.

Several of the short poems are full of sunshine. There are the pieces on the Celandine, which the poet finds "spreading out" its

> •   glossy breast
> Like a careless Prodigal;
> Telling tales about the sun
> When we've little warmth or none,—

shrinking from cold and rain, but out bright as himself the first moment that the sun may shine,—fit model for the blazing sign of the rising sun with its pointed rays. The *Green Linnet* is a poem of "spring's unclouded weather," "with brightest sunshine 'round me spread," and its two concluded stanzas are a dazzle and glimmer of bird wings and sunbeams. The *Cuckoo* babbles to the vale of sunshine and of flowers. The *Lines Written in March* are an example of Wordsworth's power of filling a poem with the sense of light and sun with the use of very few descriptive words. The glittering lake, the green field asleep in the sun, small clouds sailing, blue sky prevailing,—these phrases account directly for very little of the joyful spacious light of spring in the mountains which these lilting lines convey.

Wordsworth has not very many detailed pictures of full day, but whether he writes of it briefly or more at length, his treatment carries always a largeness, an atmosphere of broad, rich and beloved prospects. We have, for instance,

> Bright was the sun, the sky a cloudless blue,
> A golden lustre slept upon the hills,

and

> Those silver clouds, collected round the sun
> His midday warmth abate not, seeming less
> To over-shade than multiply his beams
> By soft reflection,

and, (here he is writing of woods),

> In the still summer noon, while beams of light,
> Reposing here, and in the aisles beyond,
> Traceably gliding through the dusk, recall
> To mind the living presences of nuns,
> A gentle, pensive, white-robed sisterhood.

All these descriptions show, in their different ways, the breadth natural to him. There is more colour detail in the "sweet day" on the banks of Yarrow

> while sere leaves
> Were on the bough, or falling;
> But breezes played, and sunshine gleamed—
> The forest to embolden;
> Reddened the fiery hues, and shot
> Transparence through the golden.

(Elsewhere he notes "the sunshine of the withering fern.")

Wordsworth's most vivid midday sun passage is that in Book I of the *Prelude,* telling how, as a boy, he made "one long bathing of a summer's day."—

> Basked in the sun, and plunged and basked again
> Alternate, all a summer's day, or scoured
> The sandy fields, leaping through flowery groves
> Of yellow ragwort; or, when rock and hill,
> The woods, and distant Skiddaw's lofty height,
> Were bronzed with deepest radiance, stood alone
> Beneath the sky . . .

Here are few light-words; the impression of clear and burning sunshine owes almost as much to the sandy fields and yellow ragwort as to the bronzed radiance on wood and distant hill.

Though he expressed with such feeling the splendours of the "golden light of summer," and "midday's flaming eye," it is not, of course, to be thought that Wordsworth cared only for sunshiny weather and stainless skies; but his treatment of clouds and broken light will be more conveniently noticed a little later. There is no doubt, however, that when he wrote of the day sky he oftenest made it unmistakably blue. "Blue," "azure," or "cerulean," it usually definitely is. It was "the witchery of the soft blue sky" that Peter Bell's insensibility did not feel.

The breeze seems

> half conscious of the joy it brings
> From the green fields and from the azure sky.

At Blea Tarn the wanderers stood

> beneath the concave of a blue
> And cloudless sky.

And here, says one,

> . . . . the chasm of sky above my head
> Is heaven's profoundest azure; no domain
> For fickle, short-lived clouds to occupy,
> Or to pass through; but rather an abyss
> In which the everlasting stars abide;

42

And whose soft gloom, and boundless depth,
      might tempt
The curious eye to look for them by day.

The "softness" of the blue sky of day here most interestingly becomes even a "soft gloom."

It is unnecessary to add instances which may be
found broadcast in Wordsworth's pages; especially as
this point will recur in the detailed study of his colour-
uses. Of the autumn sky he liked to use the word
"crystalline"; as in the *Guide to the Lakes*, "the atmosphere seems refined, and the sky rendered more
crystalline, as the vivifying heat of the year abates."

Momentous as was the dawn in Wordsworth's history, it seems quite clear that he loved sunset and evening even better, though he has a few lines suggesting
the contrary. Thus the *Ode to Lycoris* says, rather artificially, that it is in youth we love the darksome dawn,
prefer twilight to daybreak, and affect sad fancies,
from prodigal excess of happiness. The truth seems to
be that though dawn brought some of the consecrated
hours of his youth, his love for the close of day was at
all times the greater, and increasingly so as life went
on.

The sonnet written at Loch Lomond to the planet
Venus tells of his fuller delight in her as evening than
as morning star:

> Though joy attend Thee orient at the birth
> Of dawn, it cheers the lofty spirit most
> To watch thy course when Day-light, fled from
>   earth,
> In the grey sky has left his lingering Ghost.

The sonnet to I. F. speaks of

> The star which comes at close of day to shine
> More heavenly bright than when it leads the morn.

Beside Rydal Mere the poet writes of "the dawn of
night"—

> When the East kindles with the full moon's light;
> Not like the rising sun's impatient glow
> Dazzling the mountains, but an overflow
> Of solemn splendour, in mutation slow.

In the *Tintern Abbey* poem it is in the light of *setting*
suns that he feels the Spirit of the Universe to dwell.
A sunset forms the concluding splendour of the *Excursion;* a sunset image is the climax of one of his boyhood's poems,—(an image afterwards altered into the
metre of the *Prelude,* and used in the eighth book)—

> Thus, while the sun sinks down to rest
> Far in the regions of the west,
> Though to the vale no parting beam
> Be given, not one memorial gleam,
> A lingering light he fondly throws
> On the dear hills where first he rose.

LIGHT AND COLOUR IN WORDSWORTH

To analyse Wordsworth's sunsets in their suggestions of light and colour, we may first notice what he
says of the appearance of the orb itself as it sinks. The
following passages give us, under a different aspect,
those still and spacious skies we have learned to expect
in him:—

> . . . The sun
> When it reveals, in evening majesty,
> Features half lost in their own pure light . . .

> there [between the Langdale Pikes] the sun
> himself
> At the calm close of summer's longest day
> Rests his substantial orb . . .

> the broad sun
> Sinks down to rest in his tranquillity . . .

> . . . the fires
> Of the sun going down to his rest,
> In the broad open eye of the solitary sky[1] . . .

> All, all was cheerless to the horizon's bound;
> The weary eye . . . wheresoe'er it strays,
> Marks nothing but the red sun's setting round.

He has more to say of the radiance of the clouds "in
which the sun his setting shrouds," and of the soft or
splendid colours of the sunset sky. No one can forget
with what sad and tender majesty the Immortality Ode
suggests how the experience of life sobers, for the eye,

---

[1] These lines have to some readers (Coleridge among them) suggested
an overpowering sadness. See De Quincey, *On Wordsworth's Poetry.*

the colours of the clouds that gather round the setting
sun.

The *Evening Walk* presents, in the following lines,
the sun's orb, a cloud-picture, and a mountain illumination:

> Hung o'er a cloud, above the steep that rears
> Its edge all flame, the broadening sun appears;
> A long blue bar its aegis orb divides,
> And breaks the spreading of its golden tides.

The poet repeats this blue bar in the ode beginning
"Who rises on the banks of Seine"; the spear of Imperial France

> Seemed to bisect her orbed shield,
> As stretches a blue bar of solid cloud
> Across the setting sun and all the fiery west.

And elsewhere he tells how

> Clouds, lingering yet, extend in solid bars
> Through the grey west.

The "fiery west," above, is matched for intensity of
colouring in the phrase of the *Excursion,* where the
Wanderer saw the sun

>   toward the deep
> Sink, with a retinue of flaming clouds
> Attended—

Full of brightness too, is the cloud-sunset of the last
book of the *Excursion:*

> Already had the sun,
> Sinking with less than ordinary state,
> Attained his western bound; but rays of light—
> Now suddenly diverging from the orb
> Retired behind the mountain tops or veiled
> By the dense air—shot upwards to the crown
> Of the blue firmament—aloft, and wide:
> And multitudes of little floating clouds,
> Through their ethereal texture pierced—ere we,
> Who saw, of change were conscious—had become
> Vivid as fire; clouds separately poised,—
> Innumerable multitudes of forms
> Scattered through half the circle of the sky;
> And giving back, and shedding each on each,
> With prodigal communion, the bright hues
> Which from the unapparent fount of glory
> They had imbibed, and ceased not to receive.

We hear of the "pomp" and "splendour" of "the most
alluring clouds that mount the sky," those which

> Owe to a troubled element their forms,
> Their hues to sunset.

But more truely Wordsworthian than these lines suggesting an intense but quickly passing glory, are those
attuned to "steadfast things," which tell of

> . . . fleecy clouds
> That struggling through the western sky, have won
> Their pensive light from a departed sun,—

or of

> Islands that together lie
> As quietly as spots of sky
> Among the evening clouds,—

or of Wansfell, when along its breast

> serenely float
> Evening's angelic clouds.

In such lines we taste again the large serenity of Wordsworth's skies.

He enjoyed tracing fantastic shapes in sunset clouds; in the sonnet *Sky Prospect*, he sees in the "shows" of the "burning west," "the craggy nape of a proud Ararat"—the Ark—a rampant lion—a huge crocodile "agape a golden spear to swallow"—and a brown and massy grove receding from a town. Yet such forms and splendours impressed him as too unreal and transitory for abiding joy,—

> Behold, already they forget to shine,
> Dissolve—and leave, to him who gazed, a sigh.

The lines composed in 1802, after a journey across the Hambleton Hills, tell the same story. The poet arrived in darkness,

48

Yet did the glowing west with marvellous power
Salute us; there stood Indian citadel,
Temple of Greece, and minster with its tower
Substantially expressed—a place for bell
Or clock to toll from! Many a tempting isle,
With groves that never were imagined, lay
Mid seas how steadfast! objects all for the eye
Of silent rapture; but we felt the while
We should forget them; they are of the sky,
And from our earthly memory fade away.

The lights and colours of the after-sunset sky
Wordsworth touches with little detail, but with a happy
breadth which again shows his habit of feeling. We
have "the sky red with evening lights," and "the crimson day in quietness withdrawn"; we read how

The Sun, that seemed so mildly to retire,
Flung back from distant climes a streaming fire,
Whose blaze is now subdued to tender gleams,
Prelude of night's approach with soothing dreams,

and how

the solemn evening Shadows sail
On red slow-waving pinions down the vale.

One sunset observation which seems, in poetry, almost
peculiar to Wordsworth, is the yellow light—"the first
sweet evening yellow"—he calls it, of the long level
rays of the sinking sun. (He speaks also, but seldom,
of this yellow at dawn, as

The morning light was yellowing the hilltops).

He loves to

> track the yellow lights from steep to steep,
> As up the opposing hills they softly creep—

to mark how

> the sun declining shot
> A slant and mellow radiance which began
> To fall upon us—

to look on "turrets tipped with evening gold," and to note the weather-stains on

> The old Tower's brow, yellowed as with the
>   beams
> Of sunset ever there.

"I watched," he says,

> the golden beams of light
> Flung from the setting sun as they reposed
> In silent beauty on the naked ridge
> Of a high eastern hill.

And

> Bruges I saw attired with yellow light
> (Streamed from the west) as with a robe of
>   power . . .

The setting sun leaves all dim in the grove at Thun, where stands a memorial stone,

> all, save this bright stone
> Touched by his golden finger.

Again, the sinking sun

> had become invisible,—a pomp
> Leaving behind of yellow radiance spread
> Over the mountain side, in contrast bold
> With ample shadows, seemingly, no less
> Than those resplendent lights, his rich
> bequest . . .

The *Evening Walk* sunset, mentioned above, must now be given in full for its richness of detail, including this of the "yellow beams":

> Hung o'er a cloud, above the steep that rears
> Its edge all flame, the broad'ning sun appears;
> A long blue bar its aegis orb divides,
> And breaks the spreading of its golden tides;
> And now it touches on the purple steep
> That flings his shadow on the pictur'd deep.
> Cross the calm lake's blue shades the cliffs aspire,
> With towers and woods a "prospect all on fire";
> The coves and secret hollows thro' a ray
> Of fainter gold a purple gleam betray;
> The gilded turf arrays in richer green
> Each speck of lawn the broken rocks between;[1]
> Deep yellow beams the scatter'd boles illume,
> Far in the level forest's central gloom; . . .

---

[1] Altered later to:
> Each slip of lawn the broken rocks between
> Shines in the light with more than earthly green.

Where oaks o'erhang the road the radiance shoots
On tawny earth, wild weeds, and twisted roots;
The Druid stones their lighted fane unfold,
And all the babbling brooks are liquid gold;
Sunk to a curve the day-star lessens still,
Gives one bright glance, and sinks behind the hill.

With all its too descriptive, eighteenth century tone, this passage is highly interesting, for these redundant adjectives reveal that Wordsworth in his youth had not only a vivid colour-sense, but feelings as to certain light-effects which make their presence felt in his mature work. The "broad'ning" of the sinking sun, the reflections, the juxtaposition of light and shadow, the sun-down brightness on rocks, are matters in which his interest never faded.[1] Besides these and the yellow beams illuminating scattered boles, there is in this passage another peculiarly Wordsworthian observation, that of the increased strength or value of colour under the sunset light. Who has not noticed how, at this hour, "the gilded turf arrays in richer green each speck of lawn"? Again, in the *Excursion*, at evening when the shades of afternoon have fallen and the silvery lake is streaked with placid blue, someone exclaims, "How temptingly the landscape shines!" This intensifying of

---

[1] Hazlitt amusingly tells that when he visited the poet at Nether Stowey, "Wordsworth, looking out of the low latticed window, said, 'How beautifully the sun sets on that yellow bank!' I thought within myself, 'With what eyes these poets see nature!' And ever after, when I saw the sunset stream upon the objects facing it, conceived I had made a discovery, or thanked Mr. Wordsworth for having made on for me!" (*My First Acquaintance with Poets*).

colour and clearness, at "the tranquil hour of purpureal eve" comes out in the lines *On an Evening of
Extraordinary Splendour and Beauty:*

> Far distant images draw nigh,
> Called forth by wondrous potency,
> Of beamy radiance, that imbues
> Whate'er it strikes, with gem-like hues!
> In vision exquisitely clear,
> Herds range along the mountain-side;
> And glistening antlers are descried;
> And gilded flocks appear.

In a passage of the *Descriptive Sketches,* where
beams of evening slipping in between the mists gently
illuminate the sober scene of a remote Swiss valley,
Wordsworth notes how

> in clear view displayed
> The still vale lengthens underneath its shade
> Of low-hung vapour; on the freshened mead
> The green light sparkles.

As for mountain sunsets, most Wordsworthian is the
passage in the *Prelude* about the mountain shepherd,
when

> as he stepped
> Beyond the boundary line of some hill-shadow,
> His form hath flashed upon me, glorified
> By the deep radiance of the setting sun . . .

FOUR STUDIES IN WORDSWORTH

Of Monte Rosa it is written:

> The Alpine mount that takes its name
> From roseate hues far kenned at morn and even
>   [grows] more bright
> From unimpeded commerce with the sun
> At the approach of all-involving night.

The Alpine traveller sees how

> A gathering weight of shadows brown
> Falls in the valleys as the sun goes down;
> And Pikes, of darkness named, and fear, and
>   storms,
> Uplift in quiet their illumined forms,
> In sea-like reach of prospect round him spread,
> Tinged like an angel's smile all rosy-red.

Aloft, says the poet of the mountains around Como, at
evening,—

> Aloft here half a village shines, arrayed
> In golden light, half hides itself in shade;
> While, from amid the darkened roofs, the spire,
> Restlessly flashing seems to mount like fire;[1]
> There, all unshaded, blazing forests throw
> Rich golden verdure on the lake below.
> Slow glides the sail along the illumined shore,
> And steals into the shade the lazy oar.

---

[1] In the *Incident at Bruges,* Wordsworth notices such an effect of
light at sundown:
> It was a breezy hour of eve;
>   And pinnacle and spire
> Quivered and seemed almost to heave
>   Clothed with innocuous fire . . .

54

There is another sunset in the same poem (the *Descriptive Sketches*) when the poet will

> Seek at eve the bank of Tusa's stream
> Where mid dim towers and woods, her waters
>   gleam.
> From the bright wave, in solemn gloom, retire
> The dull-red steeps, and dark'ning still, aspire
> To where, afar, rich orange lustres glow
> Round undistinguished clouds, and rocks, and
>   snow,
> Or led where Via Mala's chasms confine
> The indignant waters of the infant Rhine,
> Hang o'er the abyss, whose else impervious gloom
> His burning eyes with fearful light illume.

Strong as is the feeling for colour in these lines, it must not escape us that the feeling for contrast of light and shade is stronger still, being indeed woven into one texture with the colour idea. For Wordsworth, in these early poems especially, often saw colour largely as brightness contrasted with dark, or blending into dimness.

Stormy sunsets are rare in Wordsworth; but there is a fine one described as following a day of rain, in the *Descriptive Sketches:*

> The sky is veiled, and every cheerful sight;
> Dark is the region, as with coming night;
> But what a sudden burst of overwhelming light!
> Triumphant on the bosom of the storm,

Glances the wheeling eagle's glorious form!
Eastward, in long perspective glittering, shine
The wood-crowned cliffs that o'er the lake recline;
Those lofty cliffs a hundred streams unfold,
At once to pillars turned that flame with gold:
Behind his sail the peasant shrinks, to shun
The *west,* that burns like one dilated sun
A crucible of mighty compass, felt
By mountains, glowing till they seem to melt.

There is one also in *Guilt and Sorrow:*

The gathering clouds grow red with stormy fire
In streaks diverging wide and mounting high . . .

But it is almost without exception the still sunset that
he celebrates, when "the crimson day in quietness with-
draws"—the "evening calm and free," the sun sinking
"down to rest in its tranquillity," amid "the gentleness
of Heaven";—"this silent spectacle—the gleam—the
shadow—and the peace supreme."

And so we come to the twilight hour which

with religious light
Blends with the solemn colouring of the night.

This was to Wordsworth at least as dear as the splendours that precede it; a fact suggested when he writes:

Evening now unbinds the fetters
Fashioned by the glowing light

56

> All that breathe are thankful debtors
> To the harbinger of night.

Even in the sports of boyhood he felt sometimes the
presence of "that still spirit shed from evening air."

The different effects of sunset and twilight on the
mind are suggested in the *Evening Walk:*

> No purple prospects now the mind employ
> Glowing in golden sunset tints of joy,
> But o'er the soothed accordant heart we feel
> A sympathetic twilight slowly steal;
> And ever, as we fondly muse, we find
> The soft gloom deep'ning in the tranquil mind.

The tranquillity of this hour soothed him, but the
changing quality of its light also spoke to his imagination, as when

> shades to shades succeeding
> Steal the landscape from the sight—

or

> When the air
> Glimmers with fading light and shadowy Eve
> Is busiest to confer and to bereave.

For "slow-gathering twilight," not dull

> as undiscerning Night,
> But studious only to remove from sight
> Day's mutable distinctions,

causes the waters to gleam, the mountains to lower, and
brings forth now, even as to primitive man, the

> mighty barrens and the gulf between,
> The flood, the stars,—a spectacle as old
> As the beginning of the heavens and earth.

The soft, still withdrawing of the light in a beautiful ancient building is the lovely opening theme of one of Wordsworth's loveliest sonnets,—the second on King's College Chapel:

> What awful perspective! while from our sight
> With gradual stealth the lateral windows hide
> Their Portraitures, their stone-work glimmers,
>   dyed
> In the soft chequerings of a sleepy light.
> Martyr, or King, or sainted Eremite,
> Whoe'er ye be, that thus, yourselves unseen,
> Imbue your prison-bars with solemn sheen,
> Shine on, until ye fade with coming Night!—

Another twilight scene of a different "solemn loveliness" is the "spectacle of clouded splendour," the "dream-like sight," from the fir-grove at evening,

>   when the steep
> Of Silver-how, and Grasmere's peaceful lake,
> And one green island, gleam between the stems
> Of the dark firs, a visionary scene!

And the poet observes how at evening, "before a rippling breeze,"

> The long lake lengthened out its hoary line.

It cheers the lofty sprit, he says, to watch the course of
the evening star

> when Daylight, fled from earth,
> In the grey sky hath left his lingering Ghost,
> Perplexed as if between a splendour lost
> And Splendour slowly mustering.

For a charming detail of the uncertain light we may
take from a much moralised poem of 1834 this passage:

> Observe how dewy Twilight has withdrawn
> The crowd of daisies from the shaven lawn
> And has restored to view its tender green,
> That while the sun rode high was lost beneath
>   their dazzling sheen.

In the passage of the *Prelude,* Book I, which tells of
the skating at evening on the frozen surface of Esthwaite, it is clear that the great imaginative value of
the experience to Wordsworth, as well as the power
and beauty of his account of it, owe at least as much
to influences of light as to the other physical factors of
motion, cold, silence, and sound, so magically trans-
muted into poetry.   The sun, he says,

> Was set, and visible for many a mile
> The cottage windows blazed through twilight
>   gloom . . .
>   the stars
> Eastward were sparkling clear, and in the west
> The orange sky of evening died away.

The boy-poet would retire from the tumultuous throng flying through cold and darkness,

> to cut across the reflex of a star
> That fled, and flying still before me, gleamed
> Upon the glassy plain.

And as he went skimming before the wind,

> all the shadowy banks on either side
> Came sweeping through the darkness, spinning still
> The rapid line of motion.

The passage is wholly Wordsworthian in the intense feeling for sound, the delight in motion, the mystic perception in which the experience culminates; not less so in the interest in light;—the windows blazing through the dusk, the orange sky of evening, the shadows, and the stars.

After twilight, the stars.

We know that Wordsworth had a favourite among them, for he speaks of "Jupiter, my own beloved star," which is elsewhere "The star of Jove," so beautiful and large in the mid-heavens. But it is of the evening star that he loves to tell:

> Then issues Vesper from the fulgent west,
> Outshining like a visible god
> The glorious path in which he trod.

The rising and setting of stars, so noticeable in a mountainous country, had a particular interest for him. One of his notes praises the situaton of Rydal Mount "as being backed and flanked by lofty fells, which bring the heavenly bodies to touch, as it were, the earth upon the mountain-tops, while the prospect in front lies open . . . so that it gives an opportunity to the inhabitants of the place of noticing the stars . . . both . . . on the tops of the mountains, and as winter lamps at a distance among the leafless trees." And in his *Guide to the Lakes* he says: "The stars, taking their stations over the hilltops, are contemplated . . . with much more touching interest than they are likely to excite when looked at from an open country with ordinary undulations."

> At evening, when the earliest stars began
> To move along the edges of the hills,
> Rising or setting—

is the heart of the opening of those characteristic verses on the boy imitating owls on Windermere. We read of the star watched "a hundred times" as it sank below Loughrigg Fell:

> Yon slowly-sinking star . . .
> Blue ether still surrounds him—yet—and yet;
> But now the horizon's rocky parapet
> Is reached, where, forfeiting his bright attire,
> He burns—transmuted to a dusky fire—
> . . . and is seen no more.

The sonnet to Venus as evening star chooses the moment of her touching the mountains.

At Calais the poet writes:

> Fair star of evening, splendour of the west!
> Star of my country! on the horizon's brink
> Thou hangest, stooping, as might seem, to sink
> On England's bosom; yet well pleased to rest
> Meanwhile, and be to her a glorious crest . . .

The "genius of Burns," he says, "rose like a star that touching earth,"

> Doth glorify its humble birth
> With matchless beams.

A characteristic passage is this:

> 'Tis Hesperus—there he stands with glittering
>   crown,
> First admonition that the sun is down!
> For yet it is broad daylight; clouds pass by;
> A few are near him still—and now the sky,
> He hath it to himself—'tis all his own!

Characteristic, for the single star appealed strongly to

Wordsworth's imagination, which set it nobly in the famous line on the soul of Milton,[1] and with loveliest charm in one of the Lucy poems—

---

[1] Wordsworth may not have intended by the star that "dwelt apart" a star actually solitary in the sky, but this idea is at least suggested, and perhaps it is not too fanciful to believe that the later phrase, "pure as the naked heavens," while not logically connected, was due to the existence in th poet's mind of this image.

> Fair as a star when only one
> Is shining in the sky.

Grasmere's church and cottages were

> Clustered like stars some few, but single most,
> And lurking dimly in their shy retreats,
> Or glancing at each other cheerful looks,
> Like separated stars with clouds between.

Its solitude was to him undoubtedly one of the peculiar virtues of the evening star.

Wordsworth's stars are usually bright, but the opening of the *Waggoner* has this charming sky-scape of a hot evening before a thunder-storm:

> the scattered stars are seen
> In hazy straits the clouds between,
> Each in his station twinkling not,
> Seems changed into a pallid spot.

In the *Pilgrim's Dream* is a dimmed star:

> That Star, so proud of late, looked wan
> And reeled with visionary stir
> In the blue depth. . . .

and in the *Excursion* there is a sullen star, dimly reflected in a lonely pool.

We may observe our poet's pleasure in contrast of light with shadow when he notices how stars blaze

when clouds are rolled away, or when he speaks of a
star that presents its shining forehead through the
peaceful rent of a black cloud, or of twinkling stars
edging black clouds, or again of the

> star that from a heavy cloud
> Of pine-tree foliage poised in air, forth darts
> When a soft summer gale at evening parts
> The gloom that did its loveliness enshroud.

Words that he habitually uses of starlight are
"bright," "spangled," "glitter" (very frequently),
"silver," (this not often), and "fresh." The use of the
last is interesting. "Bright as a star fresh-risen,"
"bright star drest in thy fresh beauty," "fresh as the
star that crowns the brow of morn," he says. And this
idea of freshness, associating itself in our minds with
that in the *Ode to Duty*, "the most ancient heavens
through thee are fresh and strong," creates for us a
sense of healing strength in Wordsworth's skies. Other
spiritual meanings that he feels in stars add to this impression. Such images as "the mild assemblage of the
starry heavens,"—or the star of eve coming

> forth to shine
> On British waters with that look benign . . .

have their moral suggestions.
To Venus as evening star, "holy star," he says, "holy as
princely,"

> who that looks on thee
> Can question that thy countenance is bright,
> Celestial Power, as much with love as light?

Such passages express the still beauty of stars, found also in the sonnet at Grasmere in which are "Jove, Venus, and the ruddy crest of Mars" reflected in the lake; and found again in the phrase

> like stars on high,
> Satellites burning in a lucid ring,

or "stars . . . as on their silent tasks they move." Most beautiful of all is the stanza

> Loud is the Vale! this inland depth
> In peace is roaring like the Sea
> Yon Star upon the mountain-top
> Is listening quietly.

"Bright star, would I were steadfast as thou art . . . still unchangeable," cried the suffering Keats, in that "last sonnet" where the star "hung in lone splendour" is "Nature's patient, sleepless Eremite." And this cry from the restless spirit to the fair and changeless light is, and seems, wholly natural. But that Wordsworth, often thought of as a poet almost exclusively of calm, of a tranquillity passing into dullness, should see the stars oftenest as restless and twinkling, holds a possibility of surprise.

Especially when in numbers, Wordsworth's stars reveal the delight in motion which the wonderful uses of stillness in his poetry must not make us forget. "Glittering," a word so curiously frequent with him, carries an idea of tremulous light; though it may be doubted whether he always intended this. In the case of stars, it would seem that he did. He has stars that "blink," as well as "twinkling" and "dim-twinkling" ones. In earliest evening "you mark them twinkling out with silvery light"; and his Daffodils were "continuous as the stars that shine and twinkle in the Milky Way." About the Langdale Pikes,

> More keenly than elsewhere in night's blue vault,
> Sparkle the stars, as of their station proud.

We read of "the glittering quire," that "white Sirius glittered"; and that

> when soothing darkness spreads
> O'er hill and vale . . . the punctual stars
> Advance, and in the firmament of heaven
> Glitter—but undisturbing, undisturbed.

In the *Pilgrim's Dream,* the Glowworm cries:

> Exalted Star . . .
> . . . with a less uneasy lustre shine
> Thou shrink'st, as momently thy rays
> Are mastered by the breathing haze.

66

LIGHT AND COLOUR IN WORDSWORTH

To the evening star the poet says, in the sonnet written at Calais,

> Thou, I think,
> Shouldst be my Country's emblem; and shouldst wink
> Bright Star! with laughter on her banners, drest
> In thy fresh beauty.

"Winking" and "laughter" are arresting words, in this sonnet, so impassioned in its love of country; and their use here is surely a significant index to Wordsworth's feelings about stars. In another sonnet, addressing the moon, he says,

> all the stars, fast as the clouds were riven,
> Should sally forth, to keep thee company,
> Hurrying and sparkling through the clear blue heaven,
> But Cynthia! should to thee the palm be given,
> Queen both for beauty and for majesty.

These lines are important, not only for their vivid expression of star-motion, but as announcing Wordsworth's prefrence for the moon. Such poetic comparisons ought not to be leaned on too heavily; but the great number and the feeling of Wordsworth's references to the moon leave no doubt that, with most people, he enjoyed her light more than that of the starry heavens.

As a boy he came to love the moon through those

local associations so all-important in his imaginative growth:

> the moon to me was dear,
> For I could dream away my purposes,
> Standing to gaze upon her while she hung
> Midway between the hills, as if she knew
> No other region, but belonged to thee,
> Yea, appertained by a peculiar right
> To thee and thy grey huts, thou one dear Vale.

What he so loved to observe in the case of the stars was also particularly interesting to him in watching the moon: her motion, both apparent, among the clouds, and actual, in rise and setting; and the contrast of her light with clouds and other dark objects.

An early poem, the *Night-piece,* is a beautiful example of his treatment of moonlight with stars. The traveller, he says, on an overcast night looks up—

> the clouds are split
> Asunder,—and above his head he sees
> The clear Moon, and the glory of the heavens.
> There, in a black-blue vault she sails along,
> Followed by multitudes of stars, that, small
> And sharp, and bright, along the dark abyss
> Drive as she drives: how fast they wheel away,
> Yet vanish not!—the wind is in the tree,
> But they are silent; still they roll along
> Immeasurably distant; and the vault,
> Built round by those white clouds, enormous
>   clouds
> Still deepens its unfathomable depth . . .

LIGHT AND COLOUR IN WORDSWORTH

The passage is most Wordsworthian, with its contrast of the small sharp bright stars with the dark abyss, the driving motion in the skies, silent in swiftness, though on earth the wind is in the tree; the infinitude of distance and depth amid enormous clouds. Other poems notice the effect of moonlight on stars;—Cynthia, he says, puts the little stars to flight, but increases the splendour of the large ones.

Again, he says:

> the inferior stars
> Had disappeared, or shed a fainter light
> In the clear presence of the full-orbed Moon . . .

The "pleasant instantaneous gleam" which in this *Night-piece* "startles" the traveller when the moon comes out of the veil of "continuous cloud of texture close," is elsewhere (in the *Lament of Mary Queen of Scots*) called

> Smile of the Moon! for so I name
> That silent greeting from above
> A gentle flash of light that came
> From her . . .

and the poet remarks, "This arose out of a flash of moonlight that struck the ground when I was approaching the steps . . . at Rydal Mount." The great passage at the beginning of the last book of the *Prelude*, describing the ascent of Snowdon tells how, as the climbers mounted through thick dripping fog, the ground appeared to brighten,—

> For instantly a light upon the turf
> Fell like a flash, and lo! as I looked up
> The Moon hung naked in a firmament
> Of azure without cloud . . .

The sudden withdrawal of the moon, on the other hand, forms the climax of that characteristic *Lucy* poem where the lover approaching Lucy's home, "all over the wide lea" watches the sinking moon descending above her cot.

> My horse moved on; hoof after hoof
> He raised, and never stopped:
> When down behind the cottage roof
> At once, the bright moon dropped,—

and the sudden ending of light and motion strikes into the lover's brain the "fond and wayward" fancy that his love is dead.

We read of the moon

> through gathered clouds
> Moving untouched in silver purity,
> And cheering ofttimes their reluctant gloom,—

of

> Sweet Spenser, moving through his clouded
> heaven
> With the moon's beauty, and the moon's soft
> pace,

of the moon,

> Crossed by vapoury streaks and clouds that move
> Catching the lustre they in part reprove—

of the moon unveiling—

> Forthwith, that little cloud, in ether spread
> And penetrated all with tender light,
> She cast away, and showed her fulgent head
> Uncovered, dazzling the Beholder's sight . . .
> Meanwhile that veil, removed or thrown aside,
> Went floating from her, darkening as it went.

And often in the gloomy east, we are told,

> The full-orbed Moon, slow-climbing, doth appear
> Silently to consume the heavy clouds;
> *How* no one can resolve; but every eye
> Around her sees, while air is hushed, a clear
> And widening circuit of ethereal sky.

We have swift motion again in the lines where

> moon and stars
> Glance rapidly along the clouded heaven
> When winds are blowing strong,—

and in these:

> With how sad steps, O Moon, thou climbst the
> sky . . .

Thou, so often seen on high
Running among the clouds a Woodnymph's
    race! . . .
The northern wind, to call thee to the chase,
Must blow to-night his bugle horn.   Had I
The power of Merlin, Goddess! this should be.

All these passages show, in varying ways, how in-
timately the ideas of motion, and of contrast of light
with shadow entered into Wordsworth's delight in the
moon.   Therefore he loved the clouded moon, remarking with sympathy, in his *Guide to the Lakes,* that
"Milton has given a clouded moon to Paradise itself!"
The moon Milton gave to an earlier poem may well be
suggested by the following:

Who but is pleased to watch the moon on high
Travelling where she from time to time enshrouds
Her head, and nothing loth her Majesty
Renounces, till among the scattered clouds
One with its kindling edge declares that soon
Will reappear . . . a Form as bright . . .

And, among scattered clouds, says the poet,

A brightening edge will indicate that soon
He shall behold the struggling Moon
Break forth—again to walk the clear blue sky.

This "edge of light" is used in a different way when

> the Moon o'er some dark hill ascendant
> Grows from a little edge of light
> To a full orb.

The contrast, also, of the moon's brightness with dark trees must not be overlooked:

> So gleams the crescent Moon, that loves
> To be descried through shady groves.

Wordsworth when a boy had lain awake on summer nights to watch

> The moon in splendour couched among the leaves
> Of a tall ash that near our cottage stood;
> Had watched her with fixed eyes while to and fro
> In the dark summit of the waving trees
> She rocked with every impulse of the breeze.

He deplores the destruction of a

> Light birch, aloft upon the horizon's edge,
> A veil of glory for the ascending moon,—

though here the tree seems rather to be irradiated by the moon than to serve as its foil.

Motion, with Wordsworth, enters often into the mysterious charm of moonlight playing on water, or glorifying objects or landscapes. Thus, under the moon,

> The garden pool's dark surface stirred
> By the night insects in their play,

> Breaks into dimples small and bright,
> A thousand thousand rays of light
> That shape themselves and disappear
> Almost as soon as seen.

We have a swan's "moon-illumined wake," and that of a boat

> Leaving behind her still, on either side,
> Small circles glittering idly in the moon,
> Until they melted all into one track
> Of sparkling light.

The moon's

> far-shot beams
> Tremble on dancing waves and rippling streams
> With stainless touch.

And

> The herring-shoals at distance shine
> Like beds of moonlight shifting on the brine.

At night, among the Italian Lakes, the poet sat overlooking

> the sullen water far beneath
> On which a dull red image of the moon
> Lay bedded, changing oftentimes its form
> Like an uneasy snake.

In the *Evening Walk* he says:

> 'Mid the dark steeps repose the shadowy streams,
> As touch'd with dawning moonlight's hoary
> gleams,

Long streaks of fairy light the wave illume
With bordering lines of intervening gloom,
Soft o'er the surface creep the lustres pale,
Tracking with silvering path the changeful gale.
—'Tis restless magic all; at once the bright
Breaks on the shade, the shade upon the light,
Fair Spirits are abroad; in sportive chase
Brushing with lucid wands the water's face.

Like his contemporaries, Coleridge, Keats, and Shelley, Wordsworth was keenly sensitive to the magic and mystery of moonlight. Probably his strongest expression of the eerie quality of moonlight is the passage in the *Prelude* telling of his meeting with the old soldier, on a lonely ascent, ₊

Where the road's watery surface, to the top
Of that sharp rising, glittered to the moon . . .

In the silence and solitude,

lo! an uncouth shape,
Of stature tall . . . stiff, lank, and upright . . .
Long were his arms, pallid his hands, his mouth
Looked ghastly in the moonlight,—

and "at his feet his shadow lay, and moved not." Here, absence of motion, silence, and solitude, are essential parts of the effect. Stillness is vital, too, in the moonlight mystery which awed the boy snaring woodcocks

75

on frosty nights upon the mountains, when, "scudding from snare to snare,"

> the moon and stars
> Were shining o'er my head. I was alone,
> And seemed to be a trouble to the peace
> That dwelt among them.

Wordsworth gives us the tranquillity of moonlight in more ordinary moods, also. "Calm in our delight as crescent moon among the scattered stars," he says, and again "bright and solitary moon, which never gazes but to beautify"; and he speaks of the "moon's fixed gaze between the opening trees." He applies to the moon such expressions as "gentle," "benign," "mild splendour," "placid cheer," "kindly ray," "clear moonshine." To him as a schoolboy, he says Cynthia showed

> A face of love which he in love would greet,
> Fixed, by her smile, upon some rocky seat.

He has still moonrises:

> When the East kindles with the full moon's light;
> Not like the rising sun's impatient glow
> Dazzling the mountains, but an overflow
> Of solemn splendour, in mutation slow.

The *Evening Walk* has a moonrise, tranquil also, but even more interesting for its wealth of colour suggestion:

the rising moon
Frosting with hoary light the pearly ground,
And pouring deeper blue to Æther's bound;
Rejoic'd her solemn pomp of clouds to fold
In robes of azure, fleecy white, and gold,
While rose and poppy, as the glow-worm fades,
Checquer with paler red the thicket shades.[1]
Now o'er the eastern hill . . .
She lifts in silence up her lovely face;
Above the gloomy valley flings her light,
Far to the western slopes with hamlets white;
And gives, where woods the checquer'd upland
strew
To the green corn of summer autumn's hue.

Finally,

the clear-bright Moon her zenith gains,
And rimy without speck extend the plains;
The deepest dell the mountain's breast displays,
Scarce hides a shadow from her searching rays;
From the dark-blue "faint silvery threads" divide
The hills, while gleams below the azure tide . . .

It will be convenient to make a slight digression, before going on with Wordsworth's treatment of colour
as affected by moonlight, to observe what really goes
hand in hand with it, the colour he gives the night sky.
Though he has "sable night with starry lustre," "nothing but the stars and the grey sky," and, of course,
other grey skies, it is surprising how often he speaks of

---

[1] When Wordsworth rewrote, and partly spoiled, this poem, he
omitted much of this colour imagery, which is not to be found in the
Globe edition.

77

the blue of heaven at night. The "dark-blue" of the lines above is only one of the instances, in the passages quoted on stars and moon, which show how he dwelt on its blueness.[1]

Thus: "the moon is up—the sky is blue"—"the moon through half the clear blue sky will go"—"azure heavens spangled with kindred multitudes of stars"—"many a long blue field of ether"—"the hue profound of night's ethereal blue"—"the [moonlit] broad blue heavens appeared to glimmer"—"brighter than the unblemished moon before her wane begins on heaven's blue coast." The phrases "long blue night," and "cold blue nights" are striking.

Two lines quoted above from the *Evening Walk* may form a sort of text for a brief study of Wordsworth's moonlit colour,—

> Frosting with hoary light the pearly ground,
> And pouring deeper blue to Æther's bound.

For here are the two properties of moonlight in relation to colour, its silvering or whitening power, for one, and for the other, its influence on colour; the moon not only lending deeper blue to the sky, but bringing out, as will be seen, colour in earthly objects as well. Many of the passages already given illustrate sufficiently the "silvery" quality; besides this, Wordsworth has a good deal to say of the paleness the moon has and creates. As:

---

[1] He has once, in the *Descriptive Sketches,* a "browner night."

78

> Mark the summits hoar
> Of distant moonlit mountains faintly shine,

and

> The moon was setting on the hill,
> So pale you scarcely looked at her,—

and

> The moon had sunk to rest
> In her pale chambers of the west, . . .

"the moon's pale beam,"—"hair" that "bristles and whitens in the moon";—all these lines, in differing ways, suggest the pallid aspect of moonlight, as do such phrases applied to the moon as "waning," "dull and red," "clouded," "wan dead light," "moon's sullen lamp," the "spectral" or "dusky" shape of the old moon within the crescent.

In the second place, the moon's effect on colour was a favourite observation with Wordsworth.
The lines

> A stain . . . as of a drop of blood
> By moonlight made more faint and wan

contrast sharply with other observations in which this light rather enriches colours.

Part First of *Peter Bell* has a moonlight scene of "soft and lovely hue." In a quarry Peter presses his way beneath the full moon, through shadows of strange shape, massy and black, to a spot

Where blue and grey and tender green,
Together make as sweet a scene
As ever human eye did view.

Beneath the "clear blue sky," "the broad blue heavens,"
is a small green plot encompassed with grey rocks,—
and Wordsworth dwells lovingly on the "green"; he
uses the word no less than six times in this passage. [It
is used fourteen times in the poem.]   Green is indeed a
colour which appears to great advantage in bright
moonlight.

The same delight in green under the moon appears in
the beautiful moonlight passage opening Canto 4 of the
White Doe of Rylstone, a green here enriched by contrasting white in the lines about the Doe herself. Here,
too, Wordsworth introduces with loveliest effect the
shadows without which he could sometimes scarcely
think of light.

Beneath yon cypress spiring high,
With pine and cedar spreading wide
Their darksome boughs on either side,
In open moonlight doth she lie . . .
. . . open moonshine where the Doe
Beneath the cypress-spire is laid;
Like a patch of April snow
Upon a bed of herbage green . . .

Beside this must be placed the description of what probably suggested the idea to the poet,—the sight, recorded

in Dorothy Wordsworth's *Journal* of a "large white dog, lying in the moonshine upon the round knoll under the old yew tree in the garden, a romantic image—the dark tree and its dark shadows—and the elegant creature, as fair as a spirit!" Another passage of interest in this connexion, from the introduction to the River Duddon sonnets, tells how

> smitten by a lofty moon
> The encircling laurels, thick with leaves,
> Gave back a rich and dazzling sheen,
> That overpowered their natural green.

Here the brightness "overpowers" colour, but without effect of pallor. But "the mellowing lustre of the moon" "who never gazes but to beautify" can cause the gaudy paintings of Tell's tower at Altdorf to become pleasing, says our poet.

Moonlight more than once lends a most important spiritual value to the poems into which it enters. Its influence pervades the fourth canto of the *White Doe*, heightening its charm to an unearthly beauty. The moon gives also their most easily appreciated poetic charm to two poems which probably no reader has ever enjoyed so much as Wordsworth did himself,—*Peter Bell*, and the *Idiot Boy*. In the latter the owl's hooting, and the moon "shining fair" through "the long blue night," enter so often into the poem that we are not allowed to forget this background of poetic mystery; and they appear at the climax of the human adventure as the sole objects noted by the hero engaged in it:

> The cocks did crow, to-who-to-whoo,
> And the sun did shine so cold!

Even in *Goody Blake and Harry Gill,* the full moon shining clearly, "the cold cold moon," does what it can to lend glamour.

In the story of Peter Bell the constant play of moonlight, changing as the hero's cruel purposes wax or wane, affects us as at once an element of natural beauty, and a pervasive moral agency, through both of which the action attains a dignity greater than its own.

If we are unable to see in these poems all that their maker saw, at least it is clear how characteristic of him is the moonlight solitude which is the condition of their being.[1] They breathe the same spell that was upon the poet from the days when he snared woodcocks on the moonlit mountains; the passion which inspired that heartfelt cry of Dorothy Wordsworth when, walking home at night, she was accompanied by Mrs. Nicholson as far as Rydale. "This was very kind, but God be thanked, I want not society by a moonlit lake."

When Wordsworth writes of clouds, he succeeds well in suggesting those aspects of them which awakened his own strong delight.

---

[1] Solitude as to human society; each, oddly, having an animal as secondary hero.

One of these, which is to our purpose, is their shadows. To his details of sunset clouds, already noticed, may be added the picture of

> Groves of clouds that crest the mountain's brow
> And round the West's proud lodge their shadows throw.

He says that a "gorgeous floating summer cloud" often makes its bounty known to labourer or traveller by the shadow that it casts; and tells of "fleet"

> shadows, over down and field
> Driven by strong winds at play among the clouds.

In the most wonderful stanza of the *Affliction of Margaret* come the lines:

> The very shadows of the clouds
> Have power to shake me as they pass.

As for light and shadow in the clouds themselves, he notices how at noon,

> Those silver clouds collected round the sun
> His mid-day warmth abate not, seeming less
> To overshade than multiply his beams
> By soft reflection,

and he evokes the brightness of clouds in such images as "gone like a pile of clouds that in cerulean ether

blazed,"—"glorious shape"—"a bright precursor to a
train . . . o'erpeers the rock"—and the sun showering
upon "that insubstantial brotherhood, Visions with all
but beatific light Enriched."
He speaks of the "mysterious laws"

> By which the clouds, arrayed in light and gloom
> On Mona settle, and the shapes assume
> Of all her peaks and ridges.[1]

The sunset clouds naturally get most of the colour
phrases; but there are delicate colour-suggestions in the
passage about clouds (not apparently sunset clouds) at
Engelberg—

> celestial Bands,
> With intermingling motions soft and still
> Hung round its top, on wings that changed their
> hues at will—

and he watched there

> the slow departure of the train
> Whose skirts the glowing Mountain thirsted to
> detain.

---

[1] He writes to Sir George Beaumont from a cottage on the coast
near Bootle, Cumberland, that the appearance of the Isle of Man "has
afforded us great amusemnt. One afternoon, above the whole length of
it was stretched a body of clouds, shaped and coloured like a magnificent grove in winter when whitened with snow and illuminated by the
morning sun, which, having melted the snow in part, has intermingled
black masses among the brightness. The whole sky was scattered over
with fleecy dark clouds, such as any sunshiny day produces, and which
were changing their shapes and positions every moment. But this line
of cloud immovably attached themselves to the island, and manifestly
took their shape from the influence of its mountains . . ."

STONE WITH INSCRIPTION BY WORDSWORTH

The verses relate to a cedar planted at Cole Orton Hall by himself and Sir George Beaumont. Stone and tree are close to "Wordsworth's Seat." (See page 260.)

He has a close, heavy wan cloud, whitened by the moon; "bright," and "silver" clouds; and "soft, the whitest of the year"; clouds luminous or gloomy; a cloud with long purple cleft; clouds in solid bars; and, as we have seen, blue bars of cloud. Of storm-clouds he has few particulars, dwelling rather on the darkness they shed. They are "a gloomy mass that loads the middle heaven," once, and, in *Guilt and Sorrow* he relates that

> The gathering clouds grow red with stormy fire,
> In streaks diverging wide and mounting high.

Nothing about cloud-appearance in Wordsworth's poetry is more poetic than the lovely passage of the *Guide* describing the clouds among the Cumbrian mountains—fleecy clouds, resting upon the hill-tops "in mysterious attachments."

"Such clouds, cleaving to their stations, or lifting up suddenly their glittering heads from behind rocky barriers, or hurrying out of sight with speed of the sharpest edge," will often make the inhabitant "think of the blank sky of Egypt or the cerulean vacancy of Italy as an unanimated and even a sad spectacle." The *Guide to the Lakes* describes the "gloomy fissure in which Scale Force descends. This spot is never seen to more advantage than when it happens, that, while you are looking up through the Chasm towards the summit of the lofty Waterfall, large fleecy clouds, of dazzling

85

brightness, suddenly ascend into view, and disappear silently upon the wind."

It is clear in many, above all in the two last, of these passages, that Wordsworth's strongest interest in clouds was in their motion. The poem *To the Clouds* is built on their "eagerness of speed," their "racing" o'er their "blue ethereal field," the "overpeering" of a rock by the "bright precursor" to another train, their "smooth motion," their "fleeing" into one gloomy mass.

Wordsworth would perhaps have written more than he did of clouds if he had not felt that their instability unfitted them to be man's "proper food." While he could read in their silent faces "unutterable love," yet his perhaps habitual feeling, at any rate as he grew older, was that, "though clad in colours beautiful and pure," "they are of the sky, and from our earthly memory fade away." It was, however, in 1842 that he wrote *To the Clouds,* a poem too rich for any adequate quoting, which must yet lend one more charm to this page; a picture of clouds

> when they lie . . .
> In listless quiet o'er the ethereal deep
> Scattered, a Cyclades of various shapes
> And all degrees of beauty.[1]

---

[1] De Quincey was most enthusiastic over Wordsworth's "cloud scenery, or those pageants of sky-built architecture, which sometimes in summer, at noonday and in all seasons about sunset, arrest or appal the meditative." And he observes "subsequently to Shakespeare these notices became rarer and rarer." "The chapter, therefore, of *sky* scenery, may be said to have been revivified amongst the resources of poetry by Wordsworth—rekindled, if not absolutely kindled." *(On Wordsworth's Poetry).*

The rainbow, always a particular inspiration to Wordsworth, was the source of one of the best and best-known of his short pieces; and in two more important poems it appears with marked effect. In the *Immortality Ode*, we hear of the coming and going of the rainbow—with the beauty of the rose, the delight of the moon in bare heavens, the fairness of waters on a starry night, the glorious birth of the sunshine—as one of the glories of the universe from which, still, for the poet, a celestial light and visionary gleam have passed away. And in *Fidelity*, the sudden suggestion of the rainbow's light and colour amid the loneliness, the "symphony austere" of crag and gloomy tarn in the bosom of Helvellyn, is the highest note of one of Wordsworth's finest stanzas:

> Thither the rainbow comes—the cloud—
> And mists that spread the flying shroud—
> And sunbeams—

one must have the whole lovely picture.

A rainbow *is* light and colour, and needs no adjectives. "Divinely bright" Wordsworth calls it once, and "radiant"; but his best phrases are "proud as a rainbow spanning half the vale" and this other:

> Bright apparition suddenly put forth,
> The rainbow smiling on the faded storm.

Rainbow effects in mist appear in the lines on St. Kilda—"lone and loved sea-mark,"

> When with more hues than in the rainbow dwell
> Thou a mysterious intercourse dost hold,
> Extracting from clear skies and air serene,
> And out of sunbright waves, a lucid veil
> That thickens, spreads, and mingling fold with
>   fold,
> Makes known . . . thy whereabouts.

This rainbow colouring of mist appears again in these lines:

> On a mountain height
> Loose vapours have I watched that won
> Prismatic colours from the sun,
> Nor felt a wish that heaven would show
> The image of its perfect bow.

And Glen Etive is, says the poet, a

> Land of Rainbows spanning glens whose walls
> Rock-built, are hung with rainbow-coloured
>   mists.[1]

---

[1] Two letters to Lady Frederic Bentinck are full of delight in rainbows. Near the Screes at Wastwater, "The ridge of it broken into sundry points, and along them, or partly along the side of the steep, went driving a procession of yellow vapoury clouds from the sea-quarter toward the mountain Scawfell. Their colours I have called yellow, but it was exquisitely varied, and the shapes of the rocks on the summit of the ridge, varied with the density or thinness of the vapours. The effect was most enchanting; for right above was steadfastly fixed a beautiful rainbow." Again, in the Highlands: "The rainbows and coloured mists floating about the hills were more like enchantment than anything I ever saw, even among the Alps. There was in particular . . . [on Loch Lomond] a fragment of a rainbow, so broad, so splendid, so glorious, with its reflection in the calm water, it astonished everyone."

After this picture we may enter on Wordsworth's treatment of mist. This is an Alpine scene of the *Descriptive Sketches:*

> Far-stretched beneath the many-tinted hills,
> A mighty waste of mist the valley fills,
> A solemn sea! whose billows wide around
> Stand motionless, to awful silence bound:
> Pines, on the coast, in mist their tops uprear
> That like to leaning masts of stranded ships
>   appear,
> A single chasm, a gulf of gloomy blue,
> Gapes in the centre of the sea—

Pines seen through mist appear again in an image of one of the *Ecclesiastical Sonnets* (XL):

> the rood
> That glimmered like a pine-tree dimly viewed
> Through Alpine vapours—

and in another passage of the *Descriptive Sketches:*

> In solemn shapes . . .
> Dilated hang the misty pines on high,
> Huge convent domes with pinnacles and towers,
> And antique castles seen through gleamy show-
>   ers.[1]

From the Cumberland coast the poet writes:

---

[1] See the *Guide*, p. 120, where in an excursion to Ullswater, "two storm-stiffened black yew trees fixed our notice, seen through, or under the edge of the flying mists . . ."

> We had another fine sight one evening.
> ... It was about the hour of sunset, and the
> sea was perfectly calm; and in a quarter
> where its surface was indistinguishable from
> the western sky, hazy and luminous with the
> setting sun, appeared a tall sloop-rigged ves-
> sel, magnified by the atmosphere through
> which it was viewed, and seeming rather to
> hang in the air than to float upon the waters.

How important a part mists play in Wordsworth's
mountain scenery the foregoing passages show. Their
vapours were to him one of the endless delights of the
Lake mountains. "The effect indeed of mist or haze,
in a country of this character, is like that of magic. I
have seen six or seven ridges rising above each other,
all created in a moment by the vapours, on the side of a
mountain, which, in its ordinary appearance, showed
not a projecting point to furnish even a hint for such
an operation." (*Guide to Lakes*, p. 29).
Again, he tells in verse how

> Yon hazy ridges . . .
> Present a glorious scale,
> Climbing suffused with sunny air,
> To stop—no record hath told where!

"Those bright steps that heavenward raise their practicable way" are the result, a foot-note of the poem [on
an *Evening of Extraordinary Splendour and Beauty*]

explains, of either watery vapours or sunny haze. The piece called *Point Rash Judgment* had its origin in the effect, seemingly, of "a thin veil of glittering haze" in magnifying the human form. The Waggoner, too, and his wain, borrowed a majesty from atmospheric conditions:

> . . . I, and all about me here,
> Through all the changes of the year,
> Had seen him through the mountains go,
> In pomp of mist or pomp of snow,
> Majestically huge and slow.

But the greatest instance of Wordsworth's use of this illusion is a passage of the *Prelude* on the Dale shepherds seen by the poet in his school-days. As the boy

> trod the trackless hills,
> By mists bewildered, suddenly mine eyes
> Have glanced upon him, distant a 'few steps,
> In size a giant, stalking through thick fog,
> His sheep like Greenland bears; or, as he stepped
> Beyond the boundary of some hill-shadow,
> His form hath flashed upon me, glorified
> By the deep radiance of the setting sun:
> Or him have I descried in distant sky,
> A solitary object and sublime,
> Above all height! like an aerial cross
> Stationed alone upon a spiry rock
> Of the Chartreuse, for worship.[1]

---

[1] Thomson, writing of autumnal mists, says:
Indistinct on earth,
Seen through the turbid air, beyond the life
Objects appear; and wilder'd, o'er the waste
The Shepherd stalks gigantic. . .
(Seasons: Autumn.)

Mist and mountains can scarcely be separated in Wordsworth's work. Leaving the heavens and their changes, we may now descend upon the mountains, following the guidance of our poet's treatment of their light and colour.

There is a great deal of mountain colour in the *Descriptive Sketches;* some appears in passages already cited, and two others are noteworthy:

> needle peaks of granite shooting bare
> Tremble in ever-varying tints of air . . .

and

> Bright stars of ice and azure fields of snow.

This poem speaks of the "fragrant mountain's purple side," suggesting thyme, and recalling the heather with which, in *Yarrow Visited,*

> The sober hills thus deck their brows,
> To meet the wintry season.

In this hue Wordsworth has also "dark empurpled hills," and "a purple steep that flings his shadow on the pictured deep." Blue appears a few times—"blue-topped hills," "blue ridge," "blue Plinlimmon," "cerulean mounts," "azure mountain tops." His hills are often "green." He has a few passages on snow-covered mountains:

> the silent grace
> Of yon ethereal summits white with snow,

> Whose tranquil pomp and spotless purity
> Report of storms gone by . . .

> Alps ascending white in air,
> Toy with the sun and glitter from afar . . .

The sonnet called *November First* tells

> How clear, how keen, how marvellously bright
> The effluence from yon distant mountain's head,
> Which strewn with snow smooth as the sky can
> shed,
> Shines like another sun,

and stands in beauty

> White, radiant, spotless, exquisitely pure . . .

At dawn, he says,

> with gold the verdant mountain glows,
> More high, the snowy peaks with hues of rose;

at sunset, in the Alps, he describes how the

> Pikes, of darkness named, and fear and
> storms,
> Uplift in quiet their illumined forms,
> In sea-like reach of prospect round him spread,
> Tinged like an angel's smile all rosy red.

However, for a poet who wrote so much of mountains, and lived his life among them, Wordsworth in his poetry says remarkably little of their colouring. That his appreciation of it was keen we know, not only from the innumerable exquisite passages of Dorothy Wordsworth's *Journals,* written in such fullness of poetic sympathy with her brother, but also from William Wordsworth's *Guide to the Lakes,* with its rich observation of mountain colour in mass and in finest detail. On the Swiss landscape, and on the English Lake mountains in summer and winter, he has observations showing both the poet's passion, and the trained eye of the man who might have been, as Wordsworth believed of himself, a great landscape gardener,—if he had not been something even better. The Lake Mountains, he tells us, have as the predominant colour of their rocky parts, the bluish, or hoary grey, of the lichens encrusting the stone. With this is often intermingled a red tinge, from the iron of the stone. Hence, when the rocks become pulverized, "the elementary particles crumbling down, overspread in many places the steep and almost precipitous sides of the mountains with an intermixture of colours, like the compound hues of a dove's neck."

Early in October the rich green of summer passes away. "The brilliant and various colours of the fern are then in harmony with the autumnal woods; bright yellow and lemon colour, at the base of the mountains, melting gradually, through orange, to a dark russet brown toward the summits, where the plant, being more exposed to the weather, is in a more advanced stage of decay." Again, "the mountains are of height sufficient to have the surface towards the summit softened by distance, and to imbibe the finest aerial hues." This last idea appears also in some lines of the *Excursion:*

> mountains stern and desolate,
> But in the majesty of distance now
> Set off and to our ken appearing fair
> Of aspect, with aerial softness clad,
> And beautiful with morning's purple beams.

But light, changing or steady, light and its complement, shade, were the real preoccupations of Wordsworth's mind in mountains as elsewhere. His interest in them appears in such details as :—

> Sunbeams, upon distant hills
> Gliding apace, with shadows in their train . . .

and

> . . . pleasant sunbeams, shifting still,
> Upon the side of a distant hill . . .

A characteristic mountain scene is this:

> . . . You behold
> High on the breast of yon dark mountain, dark
> With stony barrenness, a shining speck
> Bright as a sunbeam sleeping till a shower
> Brush it away, or cloud pass over it;
> And such it might be deemed—a sleeping sunbeam ;
> But 'tis a plot of cultivated ground,

Cut off, an island in the dusky waste,
And that attractive brightness is its own.

In a mountain vale, he writes,

                     the clouds,
The mist, the shadows, light of golden suns,
Motions of moonlight, all come hither.

We have a picture of changing lights in the lines:

           Huge Black Comb
Frowns, deepening visibly his native gloom,
Unless, perchance, rejecting in despite
What on the plain *we* have of warmth and light,
In his own storms he hides himself from sight.

At the hour "when the lone shepherd sees the morning spread upon the mountains," is shade and light "broad, clear, and toned harmoniously." Again, for a different effect, from sunless ground, beneath a sky void of sunshine

          Clear tops of far-off mountains we descry,
          Like a Sierra of cerulean Spain,
          All light and lustre.

Wordsworth several times, in different poems, observes the apparent increase in height of mountains when the shadows fall at evening. Then

> The mountains against heaven's grave weight
> Rise up and grow to wondrous height . . .

and

> High towering from the sullen dark-brown mere,
> Like a black wall the mountain steeps appear . . .

and

> He, many an evening, to his distant home
> In solitude returning, saw the hills
> Grow larger in the darkness.

These last lines are from a passage of the *Excursion,* describing a boy's communion with nature, such that "long before his time had he perceived the presence and the power of greatness;" one of the biographical passages which help to explain the growth of Wordsworth's poetic mind. How immensely important in that growth was the power of mountain light and dark must be shown by reviewing some of his epochal moments.

First, we may recall the moonlight evening when the school-boy rowed out upon Esthwaite, in the boat taken by stealth, in "troubled pleasure"; fixing his gaze upon the craggy ridge, he lustily sent his craft heaving through the water like a swan,

> When, from behind that craggy steep, till then
> The horizon's bound, a huge peak, black and
>   huge,
> As if with voluntary power instinct,
> Upreared its head. I struck, and struck again,
> And growing still in stature the grim shape

Towered up between me and the stars, and still,
For so it seemed, with purpose of its own
And measured motion like a living thing.

The boy stole home,—

                but after I had seen
That spectacle, for many days my brain
Worked with a dim and undetermined sense
Of unknown modes of being; o'er my thoughts
There hung a darkness, call it solitude
Or blank desertion. No familiar shapes
Remained, no pleasant images of trees,
Of sea or sky, no colours of green fields;
But huge and mighty forms that do not live,
Like living men moved slowly through the mind
By day, and were a trouble to my dreams.

And he thanks the Spirit of the Universe that from earliest childhood the passions that build up our human soul were for him intertwined not with the vulgar works of man, but with high objects, enduring things, sanctifying both pain and fear. Thus, too, in boyhood, his feelings for man were set upon a foundation of grandeur, in how characteristic a way!—not through any of the pomps and heroisms which usually attract boys, but through that magic of mountain lights and mists playing about the Dale shepherds. He rejoices deeply that men "before my inexperienced eyes did first present themselves thus purified, removed, and to a distance that was fit"; and declares that those who call delusion this "sanctity of Nature given to man" through these appearances, know not the truth of the spirit.

During a youthful period of "trivial pleasures," which the poet deplores, a night spent in dancing and gaiety ended in this awakening of the deeper self in the presence of the mountains at dawn:

> Magnificent
> The morning rose, in memorable pomp
> Glorious as e'er I had beheld—in front
> The sea lay laughing at a distance; near
> The solid mountains shone, bright as the clouds,
> Grain-tinctured, drenched in empyrean light;
> And in the meadows and the lower grounds
> Was all the sweetness of a common dawn—
> Dews, vapours, and the melody of birds,
> And labourers going forth to till the fields.
> Ah! need I say, dear Friend! that to the brim
> My heart was full; I made no vows, but vows
> Were then made for me; bond unknown to me
> Was given, that I should be, else sinning greatly,
> A dedicated Spirit.

It was a turning-point of Wordsworth's intellectual life when news of the death of Robespierre and the end of the Terror in France reached him, on a day whose glory of light might symbolise the radiant spiritual vision of human life which sprang from the immense relief, joy, and gratitude of this, one of his life's happiest moments:

> Over the smooth sands
> Of Leven's ample estuary lay
> My journey, and beneath a genial sun,
> With distant prospect among gleams of sky
> And clouds, and intermingling mountain-tops,
> In one inseparable glory clad,
> Creatures of one ethereal substance met
> In consistory like a diadem
> Or crown of burning seraphs as they sat
> In the empyrean . . .

—a "fulgent spectacle that neither passed away nor changed." Another passage of the *Prelude*, describing Wordsworth's ascent of Snowdon at night is memorable. The summer's night was close and breezeless, "wan, dull, and glaring, with a dripping fog." As the poet climbed, the ground suddenly brightened, a light fell on the turf like a flash, and lo!

> The moon hung naked in a firmament
> Of azure without cloud, and at my feet
> Rested a silent sea of hoary mist.
> A hundred hills their dusky backs upheaved
> All over this still ocean and beyond,
> Far, far beyond, the solid vapours stretched,
> In headlands, tongues, and promontory shapes,
> Into the main Atlantic, that appeared
> To dwindle, and give up his majesty,
> Usurped upon far as the sight could reach.
> Not so the ethereal vault; encroachment none
> Was there, nor loss; only the inferior stars

Had disappeared or shed a fainter light
In the clear presence of the full-orbed Moon,
Who from her sovereign elevation gazed
Upon the billowy ocean as it lay . . .

And in this vision of moon and mountains the poet
found "the type of a majestic intellect":

There I beheld the emblem of a mind
That feeds upon infinity, that broods
Over the dark abyss, intent to hear
Its voices issuing forth to silent light
In one continuous stream—

voices like that "roar of waters, torrents, streams innumerable, roaring with one voice," heard in that hour,
and seemingly "felt by the starry heavens."

Most sublime of all Wordsworth's visions of mountain glory is the apparition of the "heavenly city," described in the second book of the *Excursion*. The hills
"lay shrouded in impenetrable mist";—a single step
freeing the seer from the "skirts of that blind vapour,"
instantaneously disclosed the appearance of

a mighty city—boldly say
A wilderness of building, sinking far
And self-withdrawn into a boundless depth,
Far sinking into splendour—without end!
Fabric it seemed of diamond and of gold,
With alabaster domes, and silver spires,
And blazing terrace upon terrace, high

Uplifted, here, serene pavilions bright,
In avenues disposed; there, towers begirt
With battlements that on their restless fronts
Bore stars—illumination of all gems!
By earthly nature had the effect been wrought
Upon the dark materials of the storm
Now pacified; on them, and on the coves
And mountain-steeps and summits, whereunto
The vapours had receded, taking there
Their station under a cerulean sky.

No more must be given from this well-known passage; but how deep and overwhelming was the experience we learn when, at the close, he who saw the vision, with heart swelling in his breast, cries "I have been dead, And now I live! Oh! wherefore *do* I live"? "and with that pang I prayed to be no more"!

In Westmoreland and Cumberland the mountains owe much of their glory to the abundant waters that enrich every variety of scene with lake, tarn, stream, rill, or waterfall. The water is a feature of the district which delights every observer, and of course to the native poet it was always of vital importance. In his treatment of water Wordsworth sees it oftener in relation to light than to colour. A count of his phrases directly descriptive of water shows that forty-two refer to what may be called *positive* light,—brightness, gleam, and the like; twenty-seven to light in another aspect, as clearness, transparency, or limpidity. This is a total

of sixty-nine. Forty-six phrases comprise the references to colour; of these, eighteen are cases of reflection, in which Wordsworth's proportion of colour is
higher than in other water-passages. The same count
gives references to shadow, darkness or turbidity of
water the low proportion of twelve. As water is naturally noticed oftenest for ιts brightness, this point de-
serves mention chiefly because of the poet's strong attraction to shade as the complement of the light in
other fields.

Of more interest is the fact that his phrases dealing
with motion in water—as in foam, ripples, the rush of
cataracts—stand as twenty-four to twelve of passages
indicating its repose. It is not possible to separate the
light from the motion of his waters.

He loved especially waterfalls. The "sounding cataract" was one of those things which haunted his youth
"like a passion"; the "torrents shooting from the clear
blue sky" form an unforgettable member of that assemblage of sublime objects which raised his crossing
of the Simplon to the pitch of visionary exaltation. In
more ordinary mood he loves a "bold bright sky-born
waterfall," or "rill brightening with waterbreaks the
sombrous gill." He has sparkling, dancing, glancing
waves, laughing sea, eddying balls of foam, arrowy
gleams, pools stirred by insects to dimples, lakes
streaked or dappled by breeze, sparkling foam, and the
simile "purer than foam on central ocean tost." The
motion can be quieter but lovelier still, as in *Fingal's*

Cave—"wave after wave, softly embosoming the timid light." Even gentler is the Langdale rill which descended

> Diffused adown that barrier of steep rock
> And softly creeping, like a breath of air,
> Such as is sometimes seen, and hardly seen,
> To brush the still breath of a crystal lake.

The spaciousness characteristic of Wordsworth appears in such pictures as that of

> watery glories on the stormy brine
> Poured forth, while summer suns at distance
> shine—

or of a stream that "slackens and spreads wide a wat'ry gleam"; of "the distant ocean, gleaming like a silver shield"; or that which shows how

> Grasmere's peaceful lake
> And one green island gleam between the stems
> Of the dark firs, a visionary scene.

On the clearness and transparency of water Wordsworth fondly dwells. No poet could resist a "pool of crystal clearness"; but there are more characteristic things. "Calm abysses pure, bright liquid mansions" sounds really of him; still more, "pure element of waters." Here is his declaration of faith, written by the seashore, Isle of Man:

Why stand we gazing on the sparkling Brine,
With wonder smit by its transparency,
And all enraptured with its purity?
Because the unstained, the clear, the crystalline,
Have ever in them something of benign;
Whether in gem, in water, or in sky,
A sleeping infant's brow, or waking eye
Of a young maiden, only not divine.

He tells of the "sullen reservoirs" of streams,

whence their brood
Pure as the morning, fretful, boisterous, keen,
Green as the salt sea billows, white and green,
Poured down the hills, a choral multitude!

"The water of the English lakes," he says, in his
Guide, "is also of crystalline purity, so that, if it were
not for the reflections of the incumbent mountains by
which it is darkened, a delusion might be felt, by a person resting quietly in a boat on the bosom of Winandermere or Derwentwater, similar to that which Carver
so beautifully describes when he was floating alone in
the middle of Lake Erie or Ontario, and could almost
have imagined that his boat was suspended in an element as pure as air, or rather that the air and water
were one."

And these lines to six-year-old Hartley Coleridge
give us the essence of limpid waters:

Thou faery voyager! that dost float
In such clear water, that thy boat

May rather seem
To brood on air than on an earthly stream;
Suspended in a stream as clear as sky,
Where heaven and earth do make one imagery.

The brief sentence of the *Immortality Ode,*

Waters on a starry night
Are beautiful and fair

brings to the mind's eye not only the splendour of the
waters themselves, but also their power of reflecting
the glory of the heavens. Reflections in water were,
we know, an especial joy to Wordsworth. In the *Guide
to the Lakes* he makes it a great advantage of the English Lake country over the Scotch, and especially the
Swiss mountains, that the comparative stillness of the
water permits the fullest beauties of reflection. "Considering these things as objects of sight only, ... the
principal charm of the smaller waterfalls and cascades
consists in certain proportions of form and affinities of
colour, among the component parts of the scene; and in
the contrast maintained between the falling water and
that which is apparently at rest, or rather settling
gradually into quiet in the pool below. The beauty of
such a scene, where there is naturally so much agitation, is also heightened, in a peculiar manner, by the
glimmering and, toward the verge of the pool, by the
steady reflection of the surrounding images. Now, all

those delicate distinctions are destroyed by heavy floods, and the whole stream rushes along in foam and tumultuous confusion." Again, "to reconcile a Briton to the scenery of his own country," he extols the English Lakes as "infinitely more pellucid, and less subject to agitation from the winds." "During two comprehensive tours among the Alps I did not observe, except on one of the smallest lakes, between Lugano and Ponte Tresa, a single instance of those beautiful repetitions of surrounding objects on the bosom of the waters which are so frequently seen here; not to speak of the fine dazzling trembling network, breezy motions, and streaks or circles of intermingled smooth and rippled water, which makes the surface of our lakes a field of endless variety. . . . The waters of the English lakes, on the contrary, being of a crystalline clearness, the reflections of the surrounding hills are frequently so lively that it is scarcely possible to distinguish the point where the real object terminates and its unsubstantial duplicate begins."[1]

Wordsworth, who had not dwelt among Alpine lakes as among his own, does them some injustice.

[1] The poet forgets what he saw on an early tour, and described in a letter to his sister: the surface of the Lake of Como, "half of it glowing with the richest green and gold, the reflection of the illuminated wood and path, shaded with a soft blue tint."

Compare Stopford Brooke on the Lago d'Orta: "As I walked down yesterday I thought I should have cried, so beautiful was the colour on its surface, not brilliant, for the day was dull, but it was glassy calm, and there was not a tint, not the most fleeting, of the hills and banks which was neglected in its mirror. A ceaseless change played on it, and the infinite degrees of blue from deep violet to turquoise, and all mellowed into an inexplicable tenderness, would have made Dante's heart leap as he wrote the *Paradiso*." *(Life and Letters of Stopford Brooke,* vol. i, p. 258.)

A very large proportion of Wordsworth's passages
dealing with appearances of water include reflection,
and his treatment of it is always happy. He tells of
the swan

> on drowsy billows heaved
> O'er which her pinions shed a silver gleam;

of "the flitting halycon's vivid dyes, multiplied by the
amorous water;" of the soft breeze

> from before it chasing wantonly
> The many-coloured images imprest
> Upon the bosom of a placid lake;

> trees that view
> Their own far-stretching arms and leafy heads
> Vividly pictured in some glassy pool
> That for a brief space checks the hurrying
> stream;

of the mountain-ash, decked with autumnal berries, by
a brookside or solitary tarn—

> the pool
> Glows at her feet, and all the gloomy rocks
> Are brightened round her—

of waters that, steeled

> By breezeless air to smoothest polish, yield
> A vivid repetition of the stars;
> Jove, Venus, and the ruddy crest of Mars;

of the Waggon "adorning"

LIGHT AND COLOUR IN WORDSWORTH

The landscape of a summer's morning,
While Grasmere smoothed her liquid plain
The moving image to detain;

of the moon reflected from "headlong streams;" of Derwent receiving

On his smooth breast the shadow of those towers;

of one who watches a mountain brook

In some still passage of its course, and sees,
Within the depths of its capacious breast,
Inverted trees, rocks, clouds, and azure sky,
And on its glassy surface specks of foam,
And conglobated bubbles undissolved,
Numerous as stars, that by their onward lapse
Betray to sight the motion of the stream.

These varied passages show that the poet enjoyed reflections in both still and broken water. He liked, too, the contrast of motion and stillness in reflected images, the brook's "bristling rage" tempered "in the soft heaven of a translucent pool."[1] This pleasure appears

---

[1] In a letter to Sir George Beaumont the poet is justly annoyed by criticisms *"On Daffodils reflected in the Water"* ("I wandered lonely as a cloud"). "What shall we think," he exclaims, "of criticism or judgment founded upon, and exemplified by, a poem which must have been so inattentively perused? My language is precise; and therefore it would be false modesty to charge myself with blame.
  Beneath the trees,
  Ten thousand dancing in the *breeze*.
  The *waves beside* them danced, but they
  Outdid the *sparkling waves* in glee.
Can expression be more distinct? And let me ask your friend how it is possible for flowers to be *reflected* in water where there are *waves?* They may, indeed, in *still* water; but the very object of my poem is the trouble or agitation, both of the flowers and the water."
(*Prose Works of William Wordsworth*, vol. II, Grosart, p. 182.)

in two most characteristic poems. In the stanzas on Peel Castle its form is described as "sleeping on a glassy sea."

> Whene'er I looked, thy Image still was there;
> It trembled, but it never passed away.

Of the boy mocking the owls over Windermere, we are told that in the silences while he "hung listening,"

>   the visible scene
> Would enter unawares into his mind,
> With all its solemn imagery, its rocks,
> Its woods, and that uncertain heaven, received
> Into the bosom of the steady lake.

An equally characteristic passage gives, on the other hand, the vastness of reflection in perfect stillness:

> Soft as a cloud is yon blue ridge—the Mere
> Seems firm as solid crystal, breathless, clear,
> And motionless; and to the gazer's eye
> Deeper than ocean, in the immensity
> Of its vague mountains and unreal sky!

The lines on Loughrigg Tarn, in the *Epistle to Beaumont*, give to perfection Wordsworth's sense of the beauty of water-reflections:

The encircling region vividly exprest
Within the mirror's depth, a world at rest—
Sky streaked with purple, grove and craggy bield,
And the smooth green of many a pendent field,
And quieted and soothed, a torrent small,
A little daring would-be waterfall,
One chimney smoking, and its azure wreath,
Associate all in the calm Pool beneath,
With here and there a faint imperfect gleam
Of water-lilies veiled in misty steam—
　　　. . . this hour of stillness deep,
A shadowy link 'tween wakefulness and sleep,
When Nature's self, amid such blending, seems
To render visible her own soft dreams . . .

The idea in the last four lines—so prophetic, with several that precede them, of *Endymion*—grows, one feels,
out of the shadowy link and visible dream that the reflection of such a scene is.   An instance, rather ob-
scurely expressed, of this association occurs in the lines
beginning, "The leaves that rustled on this oak-crowned
hill."   In the silence of the night, the "Owlet's unexpected scream".

Pierces the ethereal vault, and ('mid the gleam
Of unsubstantial imagery, the dream,
From the hushed vale's realities, transferred
To the still lake) the imaginative Bird
Seems, 'mid inverted mountains, not unheard.

III

Wordsworth has also reflections in ice. The water-fowl

> tempt the water or the gleaming ice
> To show them a fair image; 'tis themselves,
> Their own fair forms, upon the glimmering plain
> Painted more soft and fair as they descend
> Almost to touch . . .

And another winter description tells how

> All the distant grove,
> That rises to the summit of the steep,
> Shows like a mountain built of silver light
> See yonder the same pageant, and again
> Behold the universal imagery
> Inverted, all its sunbright features touched
> As with the varnish and the gloss of dreams.
> Dreamlike the blending also of the whole
> Harmonious landscape: all along the shore
> The boundary lost—the line invisible
> That parts the image from reality;
> And the clear hills, as high as they ascend
> Heavenward, so deep piercing the lake below.

The skating passage of the *Prelude* tells how the boy sportively

> glanced sideways, . . .
> To cut across the reflex of a star
> That fled, and flying still before me, gleamed
> Upon the glassy plain.

Then there is the wonderful island which appeared in Grasmere on a winter's day, alarming the poet and his companion, who came suddenly in view of it, with the thought of an earthquake or other convulsion of nature. Larger and higher than the old island, its surface was "rocky, speckled with snow, and sprinkled over with birch trees." "At length the appearance underwent a gradual transmutation; it lost its prominence and passed into a glimmering and dim inversion, and then totally disappeared,—leaving behind it a clear open area of ice of the same dimensions . . . thinly suffused with water." The illusion had been produced by the reflection and refraction of part of the opposite mountain of Silver How.

Another illusion of reflection Wordsworth saw when walking by the side of Ullswater upon a calm September morning. "I saw, deep within the bosom of the lake, a magnificent Castle, with towers and battlements; nothing could be more distinct than the whole edifice; after gazing with delight upon it for some time, as upon a work of enchantment, I could not but regret that my previous knowledge of the place enabled me to account for the appearance. It was in fact the reflection of a pleasure-house called Lyulph's Tower—the towers and battlements magnified, and so much changed in shape as not to be immediately recognized."[1]

---

[1] Dorothy Wordsworth's *Journal* describes the reflection of the larger island of Rydalmere on a November day—"the line of the gray rocky

Perhaps as interesting as any of Wordsworth's studies of reflections is the following:

> In a deep pool, by happy chance we saw
> A twofold image; on a grassy bank
> A snow-white ram, and in the crystal flood
> Another and the same! Most beautiful,
> On the green turf, with his imperial front
> Shaggy and bold, and wreathed horns superb,
> The breathing creature stood; as beautiful
> Beneath him, showed his shadowy counterpart.
> Each had his glowing mountains, each his sky,
> And each seemed centre of his own fair world:
> Antipodes unconscious of each other,
> Yet, in partition, with their several spheres,
> Blended in perfect stillness, to our sight!

We have here a favourite colour-contrast of Wordsworth's,—white with green; this delightful picture is one of its finest examples. The colour which predominates in his reflection studies is white; a noteworthy fact, because the leading colour of his other descriptions of water is blue, used at least twice as often as grey, the next in frequency. (Such words as silver,

---

shore . . . shaggy with variegated bushes and shrubs, and spotted and striped with purplish brown heath, indistinguishably blending with its image reflected in the still water, produced a curious resemblance both in form and colour, to a richly-coated caterpillar, as it might appear through a magnifying glass of extraordinary power."

hoary, are regarded as white or grey according to their apparent meaning.)   Green, yellow, red, and purple follow in order.   The adjective "glowing," and such a phrase as "evening colours" must of course be added to the list of warm tints.   There are several indefinite expressions, as "coloured," "strife of colour," "many-coloured."   But epithets, or suggestions, of colour in water, are rather few, though the poet was assuredly not regardless of them.   No indifferent eye would have noticed as a "minuter recommendation" of his Lakes, "especially along bays exposed to the setting-in of strong winds, the curved rim of fine blue gravel, thrown up in course of time by the waves, half of it perhaps gleaming from under the water; and the corresponding half of a lighter hue;" or the streams, with water "perfectly pellucid," and "beds of . . . blue gravel, which give the water itself an exquisitely cerulean colour," or the "stately heron . . . with folded wings, that might seem to have caught their delicate hue from the blue waters, by the side of which she watches for her sustenance."

By way of these enchanted shores, we may pass to a consideration of the poet's use of colour.

II

Wordsworth's treatment of colour, in general, may be said to be on four fairly distinct planes. These originate in different poetic states, or phases, of which colour ideas are of course only one of the expressions; but a study of these, artificially isolated, may aid to fuller comprehension of the general phase. (It is rather interesting that his treatment of light shows no so distinct differences.)

These four planes of colour have certainly no hard and fast borders; and may pass into one another. They are here numbered in an order of convenience for examination; but these numbers have not necessarily any connexion with periods of Wordsworth's development.

First, then, there is a very simple and childlike, or primitive, delight in colour as a bright, or gay spot. The *Thorn* has good examples, in "the beauteous heap, a hill of moss," where are "all lovely colours that were ever seen;" "cups, the darlings of the eye, so deep in their vermillion dye;" and

> Ah me! what lovely tints are there
> Of olive green and scarlet bright,
> In spikes, in branches, and in stars,
> Green, red, and pearly white!

The scarlet cloak, twice mentioned, and the moss "spotted red with drops of that poor infant's blood" continue the effect. The "Woodboy" in *Peter Bell* holds a hawthorn branch "all bright with berries ripe and red." Wordsworth likes to describe butterflies as "crimson," or "all green and gold;" the robin is "the pious bird with the scarlet breast," or is told when he chases a butterfly, that

> His beautiful wings in crimson are drest,
> A crimson as bright as thine own.

The *Beggars* has as its high lights a cap as white as new-fallen snow (worn by a woman with "skin of Egyptian brown"), a crimson butterfly, and "yellow flowers, the gayest of the land." We feel that the poet as well as the Blind Highland Boy's mother, took pride in those crimson stockings and tartan plaid which he wore on a Sabbath day. A stanza of the *Childless Father* tells how

> Of coats and jackets grey, scarlet and green,
> On the slopes of the pastures all colours are seen;
> With their comely blue aprons, and caps white as
>   snow
> The girls on the hill made a holiday show . . .

And in the *Sparrow's Nest* we are bidden to

> Behold, within the leafy shade,
> Those bright blue eggs together laid!

This sort of pleasure in colour is scarcely found except in the earlier poems of the so-called "ballad" type; though the "negro ladies in white muslin gowns" of the

Prelude suggest it; as does the description of the moss campion in the verses in memory of John Wordsworth:

> There cleaving to the ground it lies
> With multitude of purple eyes
> Spangling a cushion green like moss—

but there is in this a larger touch.

So far, the poet appears to express completely enough what he had in mind. But on considering the next plane of colour treatment, we become conscious of a struggle (and again, here as elsewhere, the treatment of light and colour merely illustrate a general state of mind) to express something beyond what the simple phrases contain for most readers. On this plane, colour, no longer a mere adorning spot, is seen broadly as part of the poetic scene, but is still very simply treated; as in the *Lines Written in March*, where "the green field sleeps in the sun" and there is "blue sky prevailing"—or that "clear March night" of the *Idiot Boy*, when "the moon is up, the sky is blue."

"To Wordsworth," says Sir Walter Raleigh, "the very names of the simplest things that are dear to the heart, with their tender associations, conveyed an infinitely more profound meaning than all the instrumental wealth, the abstract and general terms, of a highly developed and philosophical language." Thus the simple names of colours, the mere phrases "green field," "blue sky," as also the bare words expressing light or shadow, stood to him for such experiences of a passionate sincerity as needed not the verbal adornments, or variations natural to other poets (and at times to himself.) *Peter Bell* and the *Idiot Boy* are instances of poems in which we are probably oftener conscious of the poet's struggle to communicate his poetic experience than of sharing it with him. In the former there is a very interesting use of colour phrases, chiefly of blue skies and green earth; and there is no doubt that such lines as

> To that green spot, so calm and green,

and

> Does no one live near this green grass?

and

> The broad blue heavens appeared to glimmer,

had to Wordsworth, like many another artless-sounding phrase, an intensity of meaning which we can begin to appreciate only by a very strong sympathy. Of many a reader it may be said that Wordsworth's

> soft blue sky did never melt
> Into his heart; he never felt
> The witchery of the soft blue sky.

The first use of colour, as spots, seems to have in it the germ of the second; the writing of colour for itself changing to an attempt to bring to sight that which the colour means to the poet. The third manner, or "plane," is quite different; at once more ordinary and more artistic. More ordinary, because it is in the manner of good writers in general, being the expression of pleasure in beautiful or striking colour, its balance, variety, harmony, gradation, and the like; more artistic, because the success which Wordsworth attains in it depends on power and fineness of observation, and on skill to evoke in the reader a magic of association. On this plane of colour treatment are neither bald "spots," nor struggles with the inexpressible. Each tint belongs to the poem as a whole, and has a value beyond itself, but a value which is not too difficult to discover. Contrast with the foregoing examples the following passages:

> Thou, like the morning, in thy saffron coat,
> Bright, gowan, and marsh-marigold, farewell!

and (to a snowdrop),

> Lone flower, hemmed in with snows and white as
>   they,
> But hardier far, once more I see thee bend
> Thy forehead, as if fearful to offend . . .

and

> The beetle, panoplied in gems or gold,
> A mailéd angel on a battle-day . . .

and "Autumn, melancholy wight" delighting in the daisy's crimson head when rains are on it. In the poem

To Joanna, the passage about the "tall rock" tells of the delight the poet found

> to note in shrub and tree, in stone and
> flower
> That intermixture of delicious hues,
> Along so vast a surface, all at once,
> To one impression, by connecting force
> Of their own beauty, imaged in the heart.

Here is the full poetry of red:

> The Mountain-ash
> No eye can overlook, when 'mid a grove
> Of yet unfaded trees she lifts her head
> Decked with autumnal berries, that outshine
> Spring's richest blossoms; and ye may have
> marked
> By a brook-side or solitary tarn
> How she her station doth adorn; the pool
> Glows at her feet, and all the gloomy rocks
> Are brightened round her.

The *Evening Walk* and the *Descriptive Sketches* have many very elaborate and well conceived colour passages in this third manner (the word third, having of course, nothing to do with time.) There is little in Wordsworth's later work, except portions of the *Guide,* which so testifies to colour observation and interest. The *Evening Walk,* to apply the crude gauge of number, in 446 lines contains 81 colour-words. The

passage which follows has probably more than any
other of equal length in Wordsworth:

> the rising moon,
> Frosting with hoary light the pearly ground,
> And pouring deeper blue to Æther's bound;
> Rejoiced her solemn pomps of clouds to fold
> In robes of azure, fleecy white, and gold,
> While rose and poppy, as the glow-worm fades,
> Checquer with paler red the thicket shades.

There is better poetry in such lines as these from the
Descriptive Sketches telling how

> from October clouds a milder light
> Fell where the blue flood rippled into white.

These two early poems, conventional and imitative
in manner, so unlike the Wordsworth that was to be,
are yet notable for this glowing love of colour, and
help us to understand something of what the poet
meant when he wrote, in *Tintern Abbey*, that in his
youth the colours and forms of nature in mountain,
rock and wood were to him an *appetite;*

> a feeling and a love
> That had no need of a remoter charm
> By thought supplied, nor any interest
> Unborrowed from the eye.

LIGHT AND COLOUR IN WORDSWORTH

The fourth plane of colour treatment is that in which Wordsworth, rising above the descriptive mood, at the full height of his inspiration, uses colour as something so vital to that which he images, that we cannot regard it apart. Thus in *Stepping Westward,* the sunset is merely suggested by three phrases—"such a sky to lead him on," "that region bright," "the glowing sky;" yet for our imagination it burns above the human wayfarers in glorious undying hues, more real and vivid than those called up by the most successful description.

In some of his best work Wordsworth uses colour, indicated perhaps by a single word, with an effect which is due to a sort of symbolic value which the idea lends. At the opening of the *Song at the Feast of Brougham Castle,* what power is in that phrase of the red rose!

> From town to town, from tower to tower,
> The red rose is a gladsome flower,—
> Her thirty years of winter past,
> The red rose is renewed at last;
> She lifts her head for endless spring,
> For everlasting blossoming.

Apart from all historic meaning, the phrase is the high note of the buoyant, strong-flowing passage, which is written in the key of red, the red of roses. How misplaced would be a white rose here; though Wordsworth immediately, in the four following lines, brings his melody into a larger music with the second colour:

Both roses flourish, red and white;
In love and sisterly delight
The two that were at strife are blended,
And all old troubles now are ended.

When as a boy the poet, in "an act of stealth and troubled pleasure," rowed out at night on the lake, and was dismayed by the apparent pursuit of a grim sentinel of the mountains, it was black, "a huge peak, black and huge" that "as if with voluntary power instinct upreared its head;" and this blackness paints the terror of the illusion. During the period of troubled mind that followed, "o'er my thoughts," he says, "there hung a darkness," and in the "blank desertion" of his mind, where "no familiar shapes" remained, there were

no pleasant images of trees,
Of sea or sky, no colours of green fields . . .

Here "green fields" succeed the blackness in symbolic force.

In the poet's description of his great experience of the Simplon, in the *Prelude,* is the passage:

The immeasurable height
Of woods decaying, never to be decayed,
The stationary blasts of waterfalls,
And in the narrow rent at every turn
Winds thwarting winds, bewildered and forlorn,
The torrents shooting from the clear blue sky.

> The rocks that muttered close upon our ears,
> Black drizzling crags that spake by the way-side
> As if a voice were in them, the sick sight
> And giddy prospect of the raving stream . . .

In this picture the blue of sky and the black of rock take on a heightened significance, and suggest the peace and glory of the heavens so far above the deep chasm from which they are seen, and the mysterious darkness of earth, whose shattered bones try by the wayside to explain or prophesy.

Thus, when his genius was fully awake, did Wordsworth span with a leap the gulf between "descriptive" colour and such living representations as these, transform and glorify a "spot" into the rose of Brougham Castle, and carry to a triumphant conclusion such symbolisms as those for which he struggled in *Peter Bell*.

In the great cloud vision of the *Excursion,* colour takes its intensest hue, the hue of gems, sapphire, emerald, diamond,—but these hues, with the splendour of gold, silver, and alabaster, are "blazing, illuminated, confused, commingled, mutually inflamed," "molten together," and resolve themselves into a glorious triumph of light.

It is important indeed, to notice that in Wordsworth

125

colour is often a matter of light quite as much as of hue. In his later work colour, for a poet who wrote so constantly of Nature, has little prominence, and is often rather lost in the elements of light and shade, in connexion with which it usually occurs.

At least as much is owed to them as to colour in such passages as these:

> Main ocean, breaking audibly, and stretched
> Far into silent regions blue and pale . . .

>   mid some green plot of open ground,
> Wide as the oak extends its dewy gloom,
> The fostered hyacinths spread their purple
>   bloom . . .

> Purer than foam on central ocean tost;
> Brighter than eastern skies at daybreak strewn
> With fancied roses, than the unblemished moon
> Before her wane begins on heaven's blue
>   coast . . .

> Iris, issuing from her cloudy shrine,
> Those water glories, on the stormy brine
> Poured forth, while summer suns at distance
>   shine,
> And the green vales lie hushed in sober light.

The two poems on the bird of Paradise, and that on gold and silver fishes, are examples of the poet's delicate appreciation of subtle effects of colour blending or changing in variations of light. Wordsworth's feeling as to the relative value of light and colour is suggested when, in the *Wild Duck's Nest,* he declares that no fairy-queen's

> gorgeous cell
> With emerald floored, and with purpureal shell
> Ceilinged and roofed,

is so fair a thing as "this low structure:"

> Words cannot paint the o'ershadowing yew-tree
>   bough
> And dainty gleaming Nest,—a hollow crown
> Of golden leaves inlaid with silver down.

To perceive that Wordsworth remained in his best years highly sensitive to colour effects, it is only necessary to look into his *Guide to the Lakes* (first published in 1810.) This is rich in colour observation of the most exquisite fineness. Several examples have been quoted, but another here may more fully show how carefully he studied such effects. He says, "as to the *beauty* of the lower regions of the Swiss Mountains, it is noticeable that as they are all regularly mown, their surface has nothing of that mellow tone and variety of hues by which mountain turf that is never touched by the scythe, is distinguished. On the smooth and steep slopes of the Swiss hills these plots of verdure do indeed agreeably unite their colours with that of the deciduous trees or make a lively contrast with the dark green pine groves that define them and among which they run in endless variety of shapes—but this

is most pleasing *at first sight;* the permanent gratification of the eye requires finer gradations of tone, and a
more delicate blending of hues into each other."

The winter colouring of trees, twigs, and berries, and
their setting in backgrounds of snow or dead fern or
bare rock interested Wordsworth. Dorothy's Journals
record much observation of these and other effects of
colour, in which her brother of course shared.

It is worth while to give in some detail Wordsworth's
uses of particular colours, and to note the colour-words
he employed. In the "vocabularies" of these words
which are given, occasional illustrations are noted of
striking or representative uses of the terms; but these
examples are by no means always the only uses of the
word in question.

There are words, such as gold, golden, silver, bloody,
burning, blazing, fire, pure, glowing, etc., which may
or may not be used with a colour-meaning, or may have
it even when they stand also for other ideas. These
have been listed only when they seem to have a distinct
colour value. Here readers would always, no doubt,
differ somewhat in judgment, so that such a list cannot
pretend to stand as an absolute standard. The words
"albinos," and "negro," "negress," for instance, seem
to me to be used by Wordsworth with a more definite
colour idea than usually goes with them. In his one
mention of albinos he associates them, in a spectacle,

with "painted Indians." His negroes and negresses, clad in white or decked with silver, obviously contrast with these colours their dark skins.

BLACK is fairly frequent in figurative uses,—as black dishonour, resolve, instigation, clouds of passion, blacker guilt. Some very striking direct uses are the "broad black feet" of the swan; the "black and haggard eye-ball" of the cock; the "strong black eye" with its "uneasy light" of the Matron of Jedborough; and the "sable orbs" of the "yet-vivid eyes" of the Leech-gatherer. We have seen that Wordsworth used black with great power in some of his sublime mountain passages. He painted with this colour also firs and yew-trees, clouds and vapours, smoke and storms—"London with its own black wreath," "black tempests bursting blacker still in view." It is used rarely of the sky; a "heaven of sable night" is one of Wordsworth's few skies without positive colour or light. The "black sky" of a city emphasizes a passage of the *Recluse* on the empty life of those "by the vast metropolis immured."

Vocabulary:

Black, blackened, blackening, blackens, blacker, blackest, blackness, ebon, sable, coal-black, more black than coal; jet (like beads of glossy jet), sooty, colour like raven's wings, Stygian hue, black unfathomable, blackbird, blackbird's, negro, negress. (I have not noticed "dark" and its derivatives as colour.)

Besides the "huge peak, black and huge," and the

"black drizzling crags" of the *Prelude* (and of the early *Descriptive Sketches* as well), there are the "weary hills," which "impervious, blacken near," of the *Evening Walk,* and its Alpine night, with "mountains more by blackness visible, and their own size, than any outward light;" there is also Dungeon Ghyll, with its "black and frightful rent," its "basin black and small." In the storm of the *Waggoner,*

> Black is the sky—and every hill
> Up to the sky, is blacker still.

GREY. Buildings, stones and rocks, and above all, hair, are the most frequent occasions of Wordsworth's use of this colour. He has it ten times of buildings, fifteen of stones or rocks, and no less than forty-two times of hair, or heads, or beards! As he has black hair four times, dusky (dusky-browed) and brown, each once, and "bright," "yellow" or "golden" twelve times, this fact is noteworthy. There is also the "grey line" of a path; "grey skirts of mist," and grey moss and lichens. One evening and one night sky are grey; the west is grey once, the clouds twice. Twice lakes are grey, with blue; once the water is "steeled."

Vocabulary:

Grey, glittering grey, silver grey, dusky, dusk, dusky-white, grey-beard, grey-clad, grey-haired, grey-headed.

BROWN is not much used by Wordsworth. His earliest poems have most of it. Perhaps the most interesting use is of complexions. Dark-eyed (used once) may mean brown or black. There is at evening, a "dark-brown mere."

Vocabulary:

Brown, browner, embrowned (cheek), Egyptian brown (skin), dark-brown, shadowy brown (plumage), complexion dark, hazel (eye), coloured like the soil (lips), sunburnt, russet brown, red-brown.

Brown is used of cheek, skin, and hair; dusky, once of hair; dusky-browed, once. There are brown "wood-huts" and "cottages," the swan's brown little-ones, brown iron, and "that brown ridge, sole outlet of the vale."[1]

RED. We have seen that Wordsworth got from spots and dashes of red that somewhat childlike pleasure which they give to many people, but which is seldom apparent in great poetry. He also uses reds, in varying intensity, much of mountains and clouds, especially in connexion with sunset . . . "Rosy" and "roseate" are often thus employed; but these words are particularly frequent with him in writing of the human face; and in his treatment of this we find his most characteristic use of the colour red. "Blush"

---

[1] To these should perhaps be added the use of brown in two lines of the *Ancient Mariner,* composed by Wordsworth, in which the Mariner is described as
          long and lank and brown
    As is the ribbed sea-sand.

and "bloom" and their derivatives are common with him in this connexion, and have usually a distinct colour value—as, [across] "a virgin cheek pure blushes strayed;" "her blushes are joy-flushes;" "soon fades her cheek, her blushing beauties fly;" "blushes of celestial hue" "a shamefaced blush of glowing red." "Blooming," while often a vague adjective, is also often used definitely of the colouring of the face,— thus, "the roseate bloom on woman's cheek," "a face endowed by Nature with the fairest gifts of symmetry, and light, and bloom." A "blooming boy," "a blooming Wood-boy," blooming girl, lass, lady, etc., are minor examples. But frequent as they are, blushes and bloom are rather conventional words, and Wordsworth has better ways of expressing his characteristic reds, the healthy hues brought by fresh air and sunshine to the cheeks of men and women, and especially of old men and children.

Of lands where liberty reigns, says he, "On infant cheeks there fresher roses blow." He speaks again of "the rose of infancy" that "blooms upon the cheek;" also of "rosy boys," "rosy-cheeked school-boys," "rosy prattlers," "rosy cheeks," "a ruddy quire of children," "ruddy boys," "glowing cheeks," "fresh cheeks," a "face fresh and fair to see." Michael's little son carried in his cheeks "two steady roses that were five years old." Another cottage child was "in cheek a summer rose just three parts blown." At Cambridge the poet seemed to himself to see the figure of Milton

as "a boy, no better, with his rosy cheeks angelical."
And his Lucy "looked every day fresh as a rose in
June." Young Harry Gill's cheeks were "red as ruddy
clover;" and once there is a "rosy man."

Of a grey-haired peasant we are told—"The fresh
air lodged within his cheek as light within a cloud."
Old Simon Lee, for all his age and infirmities, had still
the centre of his cheek "as red as a ripe cherry."
Walter Ewbank had "as white a head, as fresh a cheek.
As ever were produced by youth and age Engendering
in the blood of hale fourscore." In another old man,
"time had compressed the freshness of his cheek." Of
the Farmer of Tilbury Vale we hear,

> His bright eyes look brighter, set off by the streak
> Of the unfaded rose that still blooms on his cheek.

Wordsworth liked the word "streak" in describing
human colouring:

> Tenderest bloom is on his cheek;
> Wish not for a richer streak . . .

Of a pale boy he says:

> Not a tinge or flowery streak
> Appeared upon his tender cheek.

And elsewhere we learn that

> a tender twilight streak
> Of colour dawned upon the Damsel's cheek.

Again:

> Pale was her hue, yet mortal cheek
> Ne'er kindled with a lovelier streak,
> When aught had suffered wrong . . .

The convenience of the rhyme is obvious; but that Wordsworth really liked "streak" is clear; for he used it also of clouds and water. "Rosebud" and "carnation" he uses to paint lips and cheeks; he notices, too, the "deep red of cheek inflamed," and the "face red with over-toil."

So many are these allusions compared with those to other human colouring, as of hair or eyes, that we may be sure that Wordsworth felt, as indeed would be in harmony with his character, a peculiar pleasure in fresh bloom of complexion, a pleasure springing from delighted sympathy with evidences of human health and well-being and innocence. And in his mountain vale the poet, who loved his kind, not looking even in that secluded loveliness for "unruffled life," or "untainted manners," yet found it something gained,—in truth,

> A mighty gain, that Labour here preserves
> His rosy face, a servant only here
> Of the fireside, or of the open field,
> A Freeman therefore sound and unimpaired.

Industry, economy, temperance, and cleanliness, are indeed made obvious by "flourishing fields, rosy complexions, and smiling countenances," says the *Essay on Epitaphs*.

Vocabulary:

Bloom, blooming, blooms, carnation, blush, blushed, blushes, mantle, flush, flushed, joy-flushes, fresh, freshen, fresher, freshness, pink, pink-vested, rose, roseate, rosy, rosy red, rosy-cheeked, rosebud, roses, paler red, uncertain red, cherry, coral, ruddy, poppy, scarlet, military red, martial scarlet, vermeil, vermilion, gules, red, redden, reddened, reddening, red-cross, red-ribboned, red-breast, redbreasts, red-deer, red-haired, blood, ensanguined, bloody, blood-reeking, blood-drop, blood-drops, blood-stained, stained with blood, stains of blood, blood-red, rubies, ruby, crimson, crimson-spotted, crimson fire, lurid, glaring, fulgent, fire, fires, on fire, fireside, fireworks, night-fire, fiery, dusky fire, vivid as fire, glow, glowing, glowing red, burn, burned, burns, burnt, red-hot, blaze, blazed, blazes, blazing, flame, flames, flaming, flame-eyed (of eagles), rusty, russet, (red-brown, see BROWN.)

Illustrations: A blush mantled upon his cheek—red as a ripe cherry—freshen the pale cheek—fresher roses —a pair of oars in gules—mine the first blood that tinged the Trojan strand—tinged like an angel's smile, all rosy red—tinged with evening's hues—red kiln glaring bright—mountains glowing till they seem to melt—

burning (sky, west, seraphs)—the west that burned like one dilated sun—(star) that burns like an untended watch-fire on the ridge—the sun has burnt her coal-black hair.

YELLOW. Wordsworth's most characteristic yellow has been described; it is that which tinges the level beams of the setting or rising sun, and the objects they touch. Like Nature, he uses this colour oftener than any other for his flowers, associating it with marshmarigold, gowan, primrose, ragwort, "resplendent furze," and stonecrop, also with broom, that "fullflowered . . . along the copses runs in veins of gold;" with the tassels of the ash, and "pale ears of yellowing corn," besides "golden" water-lilies and daffodils. He writes, too, of

> Butter that had imbibed from meadow-flowers
> A golden hue, delicate as their own
> Faintly reflected in a lingering stream.

Yellow and gold he uses often of harvest fields—"the wheat was yellow"—"yellowing corn," or "grain"— "golden" sheaves—harvests—fields. There are many yellow or golden leaves, as "golden locks" of the birch, "leaves like threads of gold," "leaf sere and yellow on the bough," a "golden perch of aspen spray."

There are frequent examples of "gold" and "golden" where it is doubtful whether any light or colour meaning exists, as "golden" age, years, mean, lot, precepts, store of books, etc. To some readers the adjective does lend a certain light to the line; to others it is, no doubt, but an adjective of moral value. But in the *Cuckoo,* the "golden time" new-born at the bird's magic call, surely owes a radiance to the colour force of the epithet.

Wordsworth uses "gold" and "golden" often with a distinct idea of light. "Gold" is a word of higher potency with him than even his most significant "yellow;" and it is so undoubtedly because of its light-suggesting quality; thus, brooks that are "liquid gold;" or "holy turrets tipped with evening gold."[1]

The word bronzed is peculiarly used of the light of mid-day in the fine lines:

> rock and hill
> The woods, and distant Skiddaw's lofty height
> Were bronzed with deepest radiance.

"Flaming" also must be counted a yellow, so far as it is colour at all, when used of the extreme force of the sun's light, as, "day's flaming eye," "the sun's flaming chariot," pillars that flame with gold of sunlight, and "the broadening sun" that appears "with edge all flame."

Of the redder yellows Wordsworth has little. The word "orange" is used in the poems but twice—both times of sunset sky. "The orange sky of evening"

---

[1] See the *Wordsworth Concordance* for the long list of gold, gild, and their derivatives, in uses suggesting light.

dying away is a most effective part of the skating passage of the *Prelude*. "Tawny" is more frequent, but less striking in its uses.

Vocabulary:

Yellow, yellowed, yellowing, gold, golden, golden-haired, gild, gilded, gilding, gilds, gilt, fainter gold, sallow, amber, saffron, tawny, orange, flaming, bronzed, deep yellow, shining yellow.

GREEN is the colour pre-eminent in Wordsworth's poetry. It has already been shown what power the mere name of it had for his mind. "Green" is used of the earth, as "blue" of the sky, with a force of feeling undeniable, if not always fully expressed.

A very large part of Wordsworth's green is that of grass. He never tires of it: "Smooth green turf;" "soft green grass," "emerald turf," "soft green turf"— he rings the changes with unfailing freshness of pleasure. He loved the bright verdure of a grassy track between gorse and fern. "Cool green ground" is a phrase worth mentioning, because an association of coolness is rather rare with him (so different in this from Keats.) At Savona in spring he saw "smooth space of turf" sloping seaward,

> turf whose tender April green
> In coolest climes too fugitive, might even here
> Plead with the sovereign Sun for longer stay . . .
> Nor plead in vain, if beauty could preserve
> From mortal change, aught that is born on earth.

The pastoral uses of turf pleased his imagination.
"Green is the grass for beast to graze." In Poor Susan's vision, "green pastures she views." But it is in
his own mountains that Wordsworth's grass plays its
most characteristic part. As in mountain countries the
green of turf has a special value as colour, so also in
their lonely places it sounds the human note. Thus for
Wordsworth green awakens associations of man, and
of home—

> Though habitation none appear,
> The greenness tells, man must be there.

>   little fields made green
> By husbandry of many thrifty years . . .

> There is a nest in a green dale,
> A harbour and a hold—

such lines bring swiftly to the mind what this poet felt
about the relation of man to the bit of earth on which
he dwells. In such phrases as "one green field," "few
green fields," "one green island," the colour and the
singleness or scantiness unite to make precious men's
homes and holdings. The poet sees his home mountains
from afar, and to his heart

>   green vales open out, with grove and field,
> And the fair front of many a happy Home;
> Such tempting spots as into vision come
> While Soldiers, weary of the arms they wield

And sick at heart of strifeful Christendom,
Gaze on the moon by parting clouds revealed.

And of his native district he cries,

Ah! not for emerald fields alone,
With ambient streams more pure and bright . . .
Is to my heart of hearts endeared
The ground where we were born and reared.

He tells of "the smooth green of many a pendent field;" of the Solitary's dwelling at Blea Tarn, "a quiet treeless nook, with two green fields;" of a "lamb on a green hill;" of "green dales beside our Rotha's stream;" of "this green vale [Rydal], fairer than Tempe;" of the pool in Upper Rydal Park, "this glade of water, and this one green field": of a field or two of brighter green, or plot of tillage-ground, that seemed like a spot of stationary sunshine. England herself is associated with the colour of her grass and trees. Here is "the last green field that Lucy's eyes surveyed." From the boat wandering among the planets, in the prologue to *Peter Bell*, the poet sees on the earth, in contrast to the "tawny slip of Libya's sands" and the "silver thread" of the Dnieper, his own beloved land, "clothed in brightest green," a "sweet isle, of all isles the Queen." And at the close of *Tintern Abbey*, the world itself becomes "this green earth," as, in the prologue just cited it is "the dear green earth."

Linked with ideas of home, green is thus naturally suggestive of tranquility and rest. So it is in these lines and phrases:

> Nor have these eyes by greener hills
> Been soothed in all my wanderings,—

"that green spot, so calm and green,"—"the green silent pastures,"—"the quiet of the green recess" [in the hollow of a vale]. The green of churchyards blends itself in the poet's thought with their sweet stillness.

> Green is the Churchyard, beautiful and green,
> Ridge rising gently by the side of ridge,
> A heaving surface almost wholly free
> From interruption of sepulchral stone,
> And mantled o'er with aboriginal turf
> And everlasting flowers.

A "green nook, close by the Churchyard wall" is planted by the Vicar of the *Excursion* "in memory, and for warning,"

> and in sign
> Of sweetness where dire anguish had been known.

A hedge of hollies led from this churchyard to the pastor's home—

> across the vale
> The stately fence accompanies our steps;
> And thus the pathway, by perennial green

Guarded and graced, seemed fashioned to unite
As by a beautiful yet solemn chain,
The Pastor's mansion with the house of prayer.

The tranquility of green may brighten into cheer. The retreat of the Solitary in the *Excursion* with its "two green fields," is

Not melancholy—no, for it is green,
And bright and fertile, furnished in itself,
With the few needful things that life requires.

But when Wordsworth's green places are not properly described as "tranquil," they are usually something more than cheerful. "Meadows' pleasant green," "fresh green fields," "the gay green field," "joy in Kent's green fields," the "green field that sleeps in the sun" (in those *Lines Written in March*, which brim over with such springtide exultation), "a springtide of immortal green"—these phrases touch varying notes of the scale of delight. Amid the savage scene of the Lake of Uri appears a "little speck" or "scanty plot" of "smiling green." "Hope rules a land forever green" —and

Well might a stranger look with bounding heart
Down on a green recess,

an "aboriginal vale" in the Alps. The breeze brings "joy" "from the green fields and from yon azure sky;"

and undoubtedly did also from the "mountain-tops that look so green and fair." "New delights" says the poet,

> Spread round my steps like sunshine on green
> fields . . .

and, supremely "motions of delight . . . haunt the sides of the green hills."

In the *Green Linnet*, the "green array" of the bird, which makes him "a Brother of the dancing leaves," is a vital element of the bright vernal ectasy of the poem. The "bright green thorn" accents the beauty of the spot in Easedale called "Emma's dell."

There are in the early descriptive poems interesting observations of green light. The glow-worm's "harmless ray" causes "small circles of green radiance" to "gleam around," or sheds "green unmolested light upon their mossy bed." At misty evening in a Swiss valley, "on the freshened mead The green light sparkles." At sundown,

> each step of lawn the broken rocks between
> Shines in the light with more than earthly green.

In the piece on the *Eclipse of the Sun,* 1820, the light is described as

> something night and day between,
> Like moonshine—but the hue was green.

Of green water Wordsworth has little—"green sea" (twice); "the salt sea-billows, green and white;" "the greenest billow of the sea;" the "green-tinged margin" of Como, and a "sea-green river."

Vocabulary:

Green, greener, greenest, greenness, green-grown, green-leaved, green-sward, green-tinged, greenwood, bright green, dark-green, darkest green, grass-green, leaf-green, olive green, pea-green, richer green, sea-green, tawny green, tender green, emerald, verdant, verdure.

Not only does Wordsworth use adjectives of greenness far oftener than those of any other colour; he evokes in many a picture the idea of greenness without explicit colour-words. Such words and phrases as vernal, ever vernal grass, grassy, leafy, moss, mosses, mossy, moss-built, moss-clad, rich with mossy ornament, brilliant moss instinct with freshness rare, a violet by a mossy stone, greatly strengthen the mass and volume of his greens. The words *grass* and *grassy* especially carry with them so vivid an idea of greenness that Wordsworth's many uses of them add immensely to its preponderance. An attractive instance is "the grass hath crept o'er its grey line" (of a path).

BLUE. Wordsworth uses blue of water oftener than any other colour (18 times) but not very often. He has "clear lakes' blue shades," "blue pomp of lakes," "pictured mirror broad and blue," "placid blue,"

LIGHT AND COLOUR IN WORDSWORTH

"blue flood" "bright blue river," "azure brooks," "blue streamlet," "blue unfrozen water," ocean's "silent regions, blue and pale" "broad blue wave" and "azure tide." In the *Evening Walk*, the lake's

> surface breaks
> Into blue spots and slowly lengthening streaks.

His blue mountains are few. "Blue-topped hills," "blue ridge," "blue Plinlimmon," "cerulean mounts," "azure ridge," "azure mountain-tops," "azure pikes," and once, in the Alps, "azure fields of snow"—these are but a meagre showing for the poet-laureate of Cumberland and Westmoreland, and the occasional celebrator of Switzerland; especially when we realise that his mountain purples, which with some writers might stand for blue, are even rarer.

But almost constantly with him the sky is blue, and it gets the largest proportion of his extensive blue vocabulary. Blue sky, indeed, either in daytime freshness and purity, or in the depth and glory of night, is an essential part of Wordsworth's poetry. Such phrases as "heaven's blue coast," "the sky's blue caves," "blue daylight's in the sky," "the broad blue heavens appeared to glimmer," "blue Ether's arms, flung round thee, Stilled the panting of dismay"—all these create a strong impression that the poet felt a special delight in this colour. And who can forget his "long blue night," "cold blue nights," "long blue fields of ether,"

or his moon "pouring deeper blue to ether's bound":
or such night pictures as "hue profound of night's
ethereal blue"—"interminable sea of sable-blue"—"fast
receding depths of sable blue"?

The impression is strengthened by his use of the
colour at the climax of the Tintern Abbey poem—the
Spirit, which we have seen, dwelt for him in the light
of setting suns, dwelt also "in the blue sky." A further
confirmation is found in the stanza which tells of Peter
Bell that

> At noon, when by the forest's edge
> He lay beneath the branches high,
> The soft blue sky did never melt
> Into his heart; he never felt
> The witchery of the soft blue sky.

It will be observed that Wordsworth's "vocabulary" of
blue, which follows, is singularly rich in qualifications
of the colour. In a poet who never strove after words
to paint colour for itself, this fact, supported by the
unmistakable feeling of the sky-phrases, is evidence of
the first order for his love of this colour.

He has few blue flowers. "The trembling eyebright
showed her sapphire blue" is a pretty instance. The
blue flower affectionately treated in the *Lines Suggested by a portrait from the Pencil of F. Stone* seems
to be the corn-flower: a "little wild-flower" . . .

> a blue flower
> Called by the thrifty husbandman a weed;

146

> But Ceres, in her garland, might have worn
> That ornament, unblamed.

"Fresh and blue as budding pines in Spring" is a simile worth noting.

But if blue flowers are rare with him, there are a remarkable number of blue stones. He speaks of the "pale-blue rocks" of the slate-quarries; of a "sky-blue stone impressed with elfin footprints;" and the boys of the Excursion Parsonage bring in trout on a "smooth sky-blue stone." Slabs of blue stone pave the floors of his cottages, and mark the graves of his rustics; and the blue roofs of a "petty town" in the mountains of the Excursion must be of the native slate. He has a path covered with "cerulean gravel." In the *Evening Walk,* as the breeze sinks, "a blue rim borders all the lake's still brink." And we have noticed the beds of blue gravel which give the streams of the Lake district "their exclusively cerulean hue."

Vocabulary:

Blue, pale-blue, soft blue, ethereal blue, clear-blue, bright blue, sunny blue, cerulean blue, sapphire blue, dim blue, dusky blue, gloomy blue, deeper blue, dark-blue, black-blue, sable-blue, azure, cerulean, sapphire, harebell (eyes).

PURPLE. It is noticeable how little Wordsworth uses this colour of mountains. He has only "purple hills," "the purple steep that flings his shadow on the pictured deep," "dark empurpled hills" (at sunset), and "the fragrant mountain's purpled side"—this last seemingly in reference to heather.[1]

(The *Descriptive Sketches* has "many-tinted hills;" which may, of course, mean anything.)

Unless the colour, in the second of the phrases quoted, is understood to extend also to the reflection, Wordsworth, in his poetry, uses purple only once each of shadows and water.[2]

The *Evening Walk* tells how, as the sun declines—

> There, objects by the searching beams betrayed,
> Come forth, and here retire in purple shade . . .

And one of the *Ecclesiastical Sonnets* has "Ocean burning with purpureal flame."

He uses purple oftener of the sky, as, "purple morning," a sky "streaked with purple," and "purple cleft" in clouds, "the purpling east." The "purple lights and ever-vernal plains" of the early version of the *Descriptive Sketches* is probably a reminiscence of the Virgilian phrase which appears in the *Laodamia* as

> an ampler ether, a diviner air,
> And fields invested with purpureal gleams.

---

[1] Heather is also suggested, without colour-words, in the ninth stanza of *Yarrow Visited*.

In his long note to *Yarrow Revisited*, Wordsworth, describing his last visit to Scott, says, that on their return from seeing the river, "a rich but sad light of rather a purple than a golden hue was spread over the Eildon hills." In the poem we get only "green Eildon-hill."

[2] See p. 107 of the *Guide to the Lakes* for purple lights and shadows on water.

In his later days Wordsworth had a fancy for the word "amaranthine," which he used four times, always in very conventional poems, of flowers or wreaths, thus: "An amaranthine crown of flowers forlorn."

He has purple of flowers and fruit: "purple bloom" of hyacinths, the foxglove's "purple cup," the moss-campion's

> multitudes of purple eyes
> Spangling a cushion green like moss,

purple thyme, purple heath, a "purple roof of vines," their "purple clusters," "Autumn's purple crown," and the "purple fruit" of the bramble. And there are the less pleasing pictures of "a man of purple cheer," and "empurpled cheeks and pampered eyes." Again: "the turf drank purple from the veins of heroes."

Vocabulary:

Purple, purple like blush of evening, purpled, purpling, empurpled, dark empurpled, purpureal, violet (veins), amaranthine, Tyrian dye.

WHITE. Wordsworth has some special uses of white which seem to help us to a more intimate knowledge of his tastes, if not of his nature.

He has a good deal to say of white clothing. A church procession in the Vale of Chamouni impressed him with the strange harmony between the glacier-pillars, and the "white-robed shapes—a living stream":

They, too, who send so far a holy gleam
While they the church engird with motion slow,
A product of that awful mountain seem,
Poured from his vaults of everlasting snow;
Not virgin lilies marshalled in bright row,
Not swans descending with the stealthy tide
A lovelier sisterly resemblance show
Than the fair Forms, that in long order glide,
Bear to the glacier band—those Shapes aloft
  decried.

Of a portrait he says,

                    There she sits
With emblematic purity attired
In a white vest, white as her marble neck.

Perhaps the most striking use of white clothing is on
dark-skinned people—as the "Negro ladies in white
muslin gowns," and the woman of the *Beggars* with
her skin of "Egyptian brown," and her cap "white as
new-fallen snow."

He often speaks of roads and paths as white; "bare
white roads;" "the bare white lines" of dreary roads;
"silvering path;" a "hoary pathway traced between the
trees;" "path a little hoary line."

One of the most interesting of Wordsworth's tastes
is his feeling about white houses or buildings. His
views on the architecture of rural dwellings, especially
on the forms of their chimneys, were pronounced; they
were equally strong on the matter of their colouring.

He wrote on a stone near a quarry on one of the Rydal islands a warning to "think again"

> if thou art one
> On fire with thy impatience to become
> An inmate of these mountains,—if disturbed
> By beautiful conceptions, thou hast hewn
> Out of the quiet rock the elements
> Of thy trim Mansion destined soon to blaze
> In snow-white splendour,—think again; and
> . . . leave
> Thy fragments to the bramble and the rose . . .

In the *Evening Walk,* at sundown, he says

> Even the white stems of birch, the cottage white
> Soften their glare before the mellow light.

He writes to Sir George Beaumont of the church at Grasmere as "sadly spoiled . . . lately by being white-washed."

"The whitening of houses by roughcast has," he says in the *Guide to the Lakes,* "tended greatly to injure English landscape," especially at the Lakes. He admits "the moral associations of neatness and cleanliness" given by white colouring to a house. But "the objections to white, as a colour, in large spots or massed in landscape, especially in a mountainous country, are insurmountable. In Nature, pure white

is scarcely ever found but in small objects, such as
flowers; or in those which are transitory, as the clouds,
foam of rivers, and snow . . . white destroys the *gradations* of distance; and therefore an object of pure white
can scarcely ever be managed with good effect in land-
scape-painting. Five or six white houses, scattered
over a valley, by their obtrusiveness, dot the surface,
and divide it into triangles, or other mathematical figures, haunting the eye, and disturbing that repose
which might otherwise be perfect. I have seen a single
white house materially impair the majesty of a mountain; cutting, by a harsh separation, the whole of its
base, below the point on which the house stood . . .
But, if I may express my own individual feeling, it is
after sunset, at the coming on of twilight, that white
objects are most to be complained of. The solemnity
and quiet of Nature at that time are always marred
and often destroyed by them. When the ground is
covered with snow, they are of course inoffensive; and
in moonshine they are always pleasing; it is a tone
of light with which they accord; and the dimness of
the scene is enlivened by an object at once conspicuous
and cheerful."

After disapproving also the use, for houses, of the
"cold slaty colour" then much in vogue, and still more
a "flaring yellow," he concludes this passage by com-
mending as "the safest colour for general use, something between a cream and a dust-colour."

Admirable as are these principles, Wordsworth's allegiance to them sometimes wavered: but his exceptions are as admirable as the rule. For instance: "I do not mean to deny, that a small white building, embowered in trees, may, in some situations, be a delightful and animating object—in no way injurious to the landscape; but this only when it sparkles from the midst of thick shade, and in rare and solitary instances; especially if the country be itself rich and pleasing, and abound with grand forms. On the sides of bleak and desolate moors, we are indeed thankful for the sight of white cottages and white houses plentifully scattered where without them, perhaps, everything would be cheerless; this is said, however, with hesitation, and with a wilful sacrifice of some higher enjoyments. But I have certainly seen such buildings glittering at sunrise, and in wandering lights, with no common pleasure." He remarks, too, that convents hanging from the rocks of the Rhine, Rhone, or Danube, or among the Apennines or the mountains of Spain, are not "looked at with less complacency" when they happen to be of a brilliant white; but he thinks the pleasure may be due to the contrast with "the gloom of monastic life," and the general want of "smiling or attractive" rural residences in those countries. In *The Evening Walk* the poet tells also, with apparent pleasure, of the moon flinging her light on "slopes with hamlets white." And when we find him in the *Prelude* "veering round" to

> the snow-white church upon her hill
> Set like a throned Lady, sending out
> A gracious look all over her domain.

we wonder whether his taste did not also "veer," and whether the exceptions do not bulk larger than examples of the rule.

Wordsworth has many white animals. There is the description of lambs, in the *Guide:* "These sportive creatures . . . with their slender limbs, their snow-white colour, and their wild and light motions, beautifully accord or contrast with the rocks or lawns, upon which they must now begin to seek their food." He writes of a sea-mew "white as Menai's foam;" and he dwells with delight on the whiteness of his frequent swans, as the one of Locarno, with "luxuriant wings"

> of whitest garniture, like fir-tree boughs
> To which on some unruffled morning clings
> A flaky weight of winter's purest snows!

The snowy ram on the green turf (p. 114) is not more exquisite than the night picture of the *Guide* and Dorothy's *Journal,*—the large white dog, in the moonshine under the old yew-tree, "a romantic image—the dark tree and its dark shadows and the elegant creature, as fair as a spirit!"

But supreme among Wordsworth's animals is the Doe of Rylstone. This "radiant creature, silver-bright" pervades the poem like a spirit; in her whiteness is suggested the mystic beauty of another world, and that whiteness is one of the major values of the poem. The piece would be but a tale of human suffering, and loss, and endurance, without the whiteness of the Doe; with it, in those passages which so wonderfully bring it in its beauty before us, we are enabled to catch, through Wordsworth's power, some glimpses of his visionary gleam, to have sight with him of "that immortal sea which brought us hither," to become conscious, if only for a moment, of a shining reality beyond those things which our eyes behold and our hearts suffer.

See how

> the dusky trees between
> And down the path through the open green,

into the churchyard of "Bolton's mouldering Priory,"

> Comes gliding in with lovely gleam,
> Comes gliding in serene and slow,
> Soft and silent as a dream,
> A solitary Doe!
> White she is as lily of June,
> And beauteous as the silver moon
> When out of sight the clouds are driven,
> And she is left alone in heaven,
> Or like a ship some gentle day
> In sunshine sailing far away,
> A glittering ship, that hath the plain
> Of ocean for her own domain . . .

Now a step or two her way
Leads through spaces of open day,
Where the enamoured sunny light
Brightens her that was so bright;
Now doth a delicate shadow fall,
Falls upon her like a breath
From some lofty arch or wall,
As she passes underneath:
Now some gloomy nook partakes
Of the glory that she makes . . .
The presence of this wandering Doe
Fills many a damp obscure' recess
With lustre of a saintly show;
And, reappearing, she no less
Sheds on the flowers that round her blow
A more than sunny loveliness.

The beautiful passage which opens the fourth canto,
full of Wordsworth's delight in moonlight in green
places, reaches its climax of loveliness in the picture of
the "fair creature," white against the greenness and the
shadows, played on by the magic splendor of the moon:

open moonshine, where the Doe
Beneath the cypress spire is laid;
Like a patch of April snow—
Upon a bed of herbage green . . .

In Emily's meeting with the Doe, long unseen, in her
memories of it, in her wanderings with it as a companion, how the whiteness counts!

A spotless Youngling, white as foam,
Her youngest Brother brought it home.

When the daughter returns to her father's desolated
roof, among the rushing troop of deer one stops and
fixes on her "her large full eyes;"

A Doe most beautiful, clear white,
A radiant creature, silver-bright!

In this recognition, completed in "a look of fond unclouded memory," Wordsworth has shown how things
divine can work through what used to be called "the
brute creation." In the lady's moods of grief,

Oh! surely 'twas a gentle rousing
When she by sudden glimpse espied
The White Doe on the meadow browsing
Or in the meadow wandered wide!

In the wanderings again, of the lady and the Doe,[1] the
spiritual quality of the creature is suggested in its
whiteness:

Fair Vision! when it crossed the Maid
Within some rocky cavern laid,
The dark cave's portal gliding by,
White as whitest cloud on high
Floating through the azure sky.

---

[1]These innocent wanderers recall another pair, whom the poet in the
sonnet on *Personal Talk* selects as one of two objects of thought "pre-
eminently dear,"—"heavenly Una with her milk-white lamb."

White has in this poem a value which cannot be over-estimated. It not only typifies innocence and purity, but brings in a suggestion of the unearthly. The Doe, after Emily's death,

> Haunting the spots with lonely cheer
> Which her dear Mistress once held dear,

comes "gliding like a gentle ghost" to that "sequestered hillock green." But this unearthliness is something far more and other than a mere spectral quality; it is a power working for good out of the unseen.

> Thou, thou, are not a Child of Time
> But Daughter of the Eternal Prime!

cries the poet, in closing his story of the Doe. For

> Powers there are
> That touch each other to the quick—in modes
> Which the gross world no sense hath to perceive,
> No soul to dream of.

The ethereal quality of white is differently brought out in the *Sonnet to — in Her Seventieth Year,* where "the blanched unwithered cheek" and "temples fringed with locks of gleaming white" suggest one so refined to something purer than flesh and blood, that, like the snowdrops, she prompts thoughts that climb

> From desolation toward the genial prime,

or seems to be, like the moon as evening deepens, "filling more and more with crystal light."

In the lines on the procession in the Vale of Chamouni already quoted, white symbolizes solemn religious mystery. It was also definitely connected, for Wordsworth, with tranquillity. The second *Sonnet to Sleep* includes in its soothing images no colour except "white sheets of water." The association appears, too in the picture of

<blockquote>
the silent grace
Of yon ethereal summits white with snow,
(Whose tranquil pomp and spotless purity
Report of storms gone by
To us who tread below) —,
</blockquote>

and this quality enters more vaguely into much of his use of the colour.

Vocabulary:

White, whiteness, whitened, whitening, whitens, whiter, whitest, white-cliffed, white-rimmed, white-robed, white-sleeved, pure white, clear-white, fleecy-white, pearly white, milk-white, silvery white (birches), snow-white (curtains, eggs, sail, beard, ram, ridge, torrent, church) ; dazzling white, swanlike, marble (neck), alabaster, diamond, pearl, pearly, silver, silvery, silvering, silver-bright, silver-collared, frost ("frost with spangled tissues quaint"), frost-like (dews), frosting ("the moon frosting with hoary light the pearly ground"), frosty ("frosty rime That in the morning whitened hill and plain"), frosts, frost-built, rime, rimy ("plains rimy without speck"), snowy, snows, snow-clad (Alp, heights), snow, bleach (frosts), blanch, blanched, pale, pale-faced, paleness, paler, paly, pale-visaged, pallid (hands; star seems "a pallid spot"), wan, bloodless (cheek), hoar, hoary (gleams; light, walls, pathway, peaks, mist, mountain-heights, diadem of pendent rocks, etc.) (dusky-white, see grey), chalky, ghastly. (These last two may perhaps fairly be counted as white, as also Albinos).[1]

III

"The chief claim which Wordsworth advances to the supreme beauty of his home" is, says Mr. de Sélincourt, "this, made by the poet in his *Guide to the Lakes:* 'I do not know any tract of country in which, in so narrow a compass, may be found an equal variety in the influences of light and shadow upon the sublime and beautiful features of the landscape'."

How great a part light and shade play in his poetry has already been suggested, and in a measure, shown. It remains to illustrate some particularly characteristic uses.

---

[1] Numerical list of Wordsworth's uses of colour words: black, 92 ("dark" and cognate words not included); grey, 128; brown, 33; red, 310; yellow, 127 (including "gold" and cognate words); green, 345; blue, 135; purple, 51; white, 429 (including "silver" and cognate words.) Total, 1650.
See appendix for full lists of Wordsworth's colour and light words.

LIGHT AND COLOUR IN WORDSWORTH

Many of the passages which have been quoted in other connections show his strong instinct for light and shade in contrast. It almost seems that he had moods when he could scarcely conceive an idea of the one without immediately associating it with its opposite. His treatment of such contrast ranges from a sort of primitive pleasure (like his elementary mode of colour-expression) in the simple shock of extremes,[1] as in the "ebon car" of the Egyptian Maid, on which "diffused like snow the Damsel lay," through commonplace like the

> vision of a lovely Maid
> Seated alone beneath a darksome tree,
> Whose fondly-overhanging canopy
> Set off her brightness with a pleasing shade,

---

[1] Wordsworth particularly affected small points of light shining through darkness: especially the two items of glow-worms, and candles or lamps. His glow-worms form a considerable company, and he always shows a fresh pleasure in them. His tapers, shining or glimmering through the dark are quite surprisingly numerous. Though he did frequently permit himself a hermit's taper, still this sort of light is oftener no mere adornment, but an honest household candle or lamp, which becomes that very Wordsworthian thing, a symbol and sign of home, stirring the heart and guiding the way of the traveller in darkness.

> Dark on my road the autumnal evening fell.
> And night succeeded with unusual gloom,
> So hazardous that feet and hands became
> Guides better than mine eyes—until a light
> High in the gloom appeared . . .
> I looked with steadiness as sailors look
> On the north star, or watch-tower's distant lamp,
> And saw the light—now fixed—and shifting now—
> Not like a dancing meteor, but in line
> Of never-varying motion to and fro . . .

And the Wanderer safely reached a mountain cottage, guided "by that unwearied signal, kenned afar," a lantern in the hands of the wife awaiting her husband. (*Ex.* Bk. 5).

to exquisite appreciation of the subtlest modulation, the richest variety, of light and shade over wide landscape. Thus, in the *Guide,* he writes of stormy weather, "Insensible must he be who would not congratulate himself upon the bold bursts of sunshine, the descending vapours, wandering lights and shadows . . . with which broken weather in a mountainous region is accompanied." There, in autumn, he tells us, "the atmosphere seems refined, and the sky rendered more crystalline . . . the lights and shadows are more delicate." And there "showers, darkening, or brightening, as they fly from hill to hill, are not less grateful to the eye than finely interwoven passages of gay and sad music are touching to the ear."[1] In the poem *Composed during a Storm* is a striking contrast: the beholder is "soul-smitten" on looking up in the darkness to see

> Large space ('mid dreadful clouds) of purest sky
> An azure disc—shield of Tranquillity.

Such a "portal in the sky" he paints again—

> Brighter than brightest loophole, in a storm,
> Opening before the sun's triumphant eye.

---

[1] Compare with this the sentiments of Wordsworth's contemporary writer on the picturesque, William Gilpin. "False shadows," he calls the shadows of flying clouds, remarking that "scarce anything gives higher offence to the picturesque eye." "In *flat* countries these *false shadows* are rarely disgusting" (being lost or broken, or altered by perspective), but "patched against the side of a mountain, and held up to the eye in their full size and dimensions, they are almost ever accompanied with great confusion." Thus, a day with sunshine and wind and small floating clouds is "the worst kind of weather for visiting a mountainous country." (*Observations in Scotland,* II, 152-3).

LIGHT AND COLOUR IN WORDSWORTH

Wordsworth's instinct for the spacious prompted him to like broad effects of light and shade in his treatment of mountains, waters, and wide landscapes. He rejoiced "in lights and shades"

> That marched and countermarched about the hills
> In glorious apparition.

He speaks of "the sudden charm which accidents of light and shade, which moonlight or sunset diffused over a known and familiar landscape." "How lovely," he exclaims of Savona,

> robed in forenoon light and shade
> Each ministering to each, didst thou appear.

At evening, by Esthwaite Water, he tells how

> the shores
> And heights meanwhile were slowly overspread
> With darkness, and before a rippling breeze
> The long lake lengthened out its hoary line.

And an even more beautiful picture is given us when

> the ample moon
> In the deep stillness of a summer even
> Rising behind a thick and lofty grove,
> Burns, like an unconsuming fire of light,
> In the green trees; and, kindling on all sides

Their leafy umbrage, turns the dusky veil
Into a substance glorious as her own,
Yea, with her own incorporate, by power
Capacious and serene.

Wordsworth loved the dark lines or masses of trees
contrasted with the radiance of the sky, as when

. . . fronting the bright west in stronger lines
The oak its dark'ning boughs and foliage twines.[1]

He writes of the pine of Monte Mario—

I saw far off the dark top of a Pine
Look like a cloud—a slender tie the stem
That bound it to its native earth—poised high
'Mid evening hues, along the horizon line,
Striving in peace each other to outshine—

and the tree, with associations of home and friendship,
and "with its sky so bright, and cloud-like beauty," for
him "supplanted the whole majesty of Rome."

Wordsworth's close observation of effects of light
appears in his lines on the eclipse of the sun, 1820.
The sky, he says, was without mist or cloud:

The sky an azure field displayed;
'Twas sunlight sheathed and gently charmed,

---

[1] "This is feebly and imperfectly expressed"; wrote the poet, but "the moment was important in my poetical history; for I date from it my consciousness of the infinite variety of material appearances which had been unnoticed by the poets . . . and I made a resolution to supply in some degree the deficiency. I could not have been at that time above 14 years of age."

Of all its sparkling rays disarmed,
And as in slumber laid,—
Or something night and day between,
Like moonshine—but the hue was green;
Still moonshine, without shadow . . .

Another piece of detailed observation is interesting,—
a sentence of the *Guide to the Lakes* which tells us that
there "the atmosphere . . . as in every country subject
to much rain, is frequently unfavorable to landscape,
especially when keen winds succeed the rain which are
apt to produce coldness, spottiness, and an unmeaning
or repulsive detail in the distance;—a sunless frost,
under a canopy of leaden and shapeless clouds, is, as
far as it allows things to be seen, equally disagree-
able."

How rich the *Guide* is in light and shade may be
seen from pictures like the following: the soft strong
green of grassy slopes in sunlight, dimmed by the
shadow of a passing cloud; flying cloud-spots; purple
crags among verdure, crimson in the rays of the setting
sun; the ridges and angles of mountains covered with
bracken, tender green diversified with patches of wintry
russet, lighted up with sudden sunlight, dappled spots
on mountain-flanks; solemn soft gloom of shadow en-
veloping a whole mountain; soft vague shadow on the
brow of a green hill; in dull weather, ridges and folds
of gloom; distant peaks of smoky pearl.

We have remarked that colour often presented itself
to Wordsworth as light, or light and shade, rather than

purely as colour. This tendency is very clearly shown in many passages which express delight in the play of light and shade—such play as Spenser loved, making "a sunshine in a shady place," or Keats, when he painted Lamia changing from snake to woman. Thus in the poems on *Gold and Silver Fishes,* the colours of the fishes are indistinguishably blent with their brightness and motion. In their "glassy prison" play "golden flash and silver gleam;" "the golden Power" casts "gleams by the richest jewel unsurpast;" sensitive to every ray smiting their tiny sea, their "scaly panoplies repay the loan with usury." They are magnified by the glass to

> Fays, Genii of gigantic size!
> And now, in twilight dim,
> Clustered like constellated eyes,
> In wings of Cherubim,
> When the fierce orbs abate their glare . . .

And, the poet declares,

> Not alone by colours bright
>   Are ye to heaven allied.
> When, like essential Forms of light,
>   Ye mingle or divide.

Of a parrot Wordsworth writes:

> Her plumy mantle's living hues
> In mass opposed to mass
> Outshine the splendour that imbues
> The robes of pictured glass,—

He has a bird of Paradise:

> With a divinity of colour, drest
> In all her brightness, from the dancing crest
> Far as the last gleam of the filmy train
> Green, sable, shining yellow, shadowy brown,
> Tints softly with each other blended,
> Hues doubtfully begun and ended;
> Or intershooting, and to sight
> Lost and recovered, as the rays of light
> Glance on the conscious plumes touched here and
> there . . .

Swans, whose "plumes of dusky white" changed, on approaching the light, their hue, like clouds of sunset, into "lucid amber," are another instance. And in the *Prelude* we read of "Gehol's matchless gardens," with their shady dells and sunny mounts, their

> groves of foliage taught to melt
> Into each other their obsequious hues,
> Vanished and vanishing in subtle chase,
> Too fine to be pursued; or standing forth
> In no discordant opposition, strong
> And gorgeous as the colours side by side
> Bedded among rich plumes of tropic birds.

The description of the *Parsonage*, in the *Excursion*, shows an exact notice of light values in beds and banks of gay flowers:

Profusion bright! and every flower assuming
A more than natural vividness of hue,
From unaffected contrast with the gloom
Of sober cypress, and the darker foil
Of yew . . .

The greater Alpine lakes exhibit, Wordsworth says,
"those ever-changing fields of green, blue, or purple
shadows, or lights (one scarcely knows which to name
them) that call to mind a sea-prospect . . ."

This interest in the changing frontiers of bright and
sombre, in the interplay of gleam and hue with dusk
and darkness, the "struggles of gloom and sunshine,"
taught Wordsworth the magic of shadows. He is not
a poet of the dark—his night, we have seen, is normally blue, not black; of gloom unrelieved he has little,
and the poem of the *Yew-trees* is the only one important for its darkness. But a poet of shadows he em-
phatically is. His observation of them, their shapes
and their motions, furnishes a lovely stuff of poetry of
which other poets have made no such detailed use.

In this "dear delightful land of verdure, shower, and
gleam," to adopt a phrase of his own, he shows us, now
an old grey stone, protected by concentred hazels from
the ray of noontide suns, where yet the beams play and
glance, while wantonly the rough wind blows;—now
the green linnet, brother of the dancing leaves, deceiv-
ing the sight as he perches in twinkling hazels, where
the flutter of his wings

Upon his back and body flings
Shadows and sunny glimmerings
That cover him all over.

Or we hear of the "sunshiny shade" of apple-trees in bloom; of "the shadow-casting race of trees;" of "dappled turf;" of a "lawn, a carpet all alive with shadows flung from leaves—to strive in dance, amid a press of sunshine;" of the "dark shadows of the summer leaves" that "danced in the breeze, chequering" the mossy cottage roof. We hear, too, of cloud-shadows; of sunbeams gliding apace on distant hills with shadows in their train; of the gorgeous summer floating cloud, whose presence is made known by sunburnt traveler or stooping labourer by the bounty of the shadow round him thrown; or of him on whom death fell "like a shadow thrown softly and lightly from a passing cloud" while lying "for noontide solace on the summer grass, the warm lap of his mother earth." The imaginative quality of these cloud-shadows rises to full Wordsworthian power in the tenth stanza of the *Affliction of Margaret:*

The very shadows of the clouds
Have power to shake me as they pass.

It is interesting to see, in those dreary *Lines Written in the Album of the Countess of Lonsdale,* lines beginning

Lady! a Pen (perhaps with thy regard,
Among the Favoured, favoured not the least)

(alas! his own)—how even from this weary tribute of
"admiration and respectful love," Wordsworth springs
up from his dull November flats of 1834, with one
awakening simile:

Fleet as the shadows, over down or field,
Driven by strong winds at play among the
    clouds . . .

Poetry welled up in him at the mere thought of driving
light and shade, as may be divined from certain lines of
the *Prelude:*

            my favourite grove,
Tossing in sunshine its dark boughs aloft,
As if to make the strong wind visible,
Wakes in me agitations like its own,
A spirit friendly to the Poet's task.

These lines of the *Recluse* suggest a similar idea; they
recall Keats' joy in grain rippling in the wind:

            breezes that delight
To play on water, or in endless chase
Pursue each other through the yielding plain
Of grass or corn, over and through and through,
In billow after billow, evermore
Disporting . . .

As we may feel Wordsworth's purest spirit of joy informing some of these shadow-passages, so possibly these on daisy-shadows had their source in another characteristic mood. That "humblest friend," the Daisy,

> by the shadow that it casts
> Protects the lingering dew-drop from the sun.

And again, the poet wishes that flowers might know half the pleasure they give,

> That to this mountain-daisy's self were known
> The beauty of its star-shaped shadow, thrown
> On the smooth surface of this naked stone!

and that even the sun might

> ken how by his sovereign aid
> These delicate companionships are made;
> And how he rules the pomp of light and shade.

Though Wordsworth ruthlessly moralises these delicate companionships, and in the bleak piety of 1845 quells the "vain desires" and "lawless wishes" of the second passage, one feels that they sprang perhaps from that deeper mind, now lost or bewildered, to which "the meanest flower that blows" could give "thoughts that do often lie too deep for tears."

A passage that, like these on the daisy, betrays Wordsworth's love of shadow shapes, tells of a

> tall pine, the shadow of whose bare
> And slender stem, while here I sat at eve,
> Oft stretches toward me like a long straight path
> Traced faintly in the greensward.

As Peter Bell entered the quarry,

> shadows of strange shapes,
> Massy and black, before him lay.

The mansion of the Pastor in the *Excursion* shows how architectural shadow interested the poet: it was

> a reverend pile
> With bold projections and recesses deep;
> Shadowy, yet gay and lightsome as it stood
> Fronting the noontide sun.

And in the *Guide* he mentions as a charm of the dwellings of the dalesmen, so wild and beautiful in their situation and form, that "Among the numerous recesses and projections in the walls and in the different stages of the roofs, are seen bold and harmonious effects of contrasted sunshine and shadow."

The "curious traveller" who with torches explores some huge cave, see above him, says the poet,

> Substance and shadow, light and darkness, all
> Commingled, making up a canopy
> Of shapes and forms and tendencies to shape
> That shift and vanish, change and interchange
> Like spectres,—ferment silent and sublime!

This recalls the more beautiful picture of King's College Chapel—its

> branching roof
> Self-poised, and scooped into ten thousand cells,
> Where light and shade repose . . .

In one of the Duddon Sonnets is

> that embattled House, whose mossy keep,
> Flung from yon cliff a shadow large and cold.

A lovely shadow, with an added charm of colour, is that of *Ecclesiastical Sonnet 27* (Part I) :

> 'mid some green plot of open ground
> Wide as the oak extends its dewy gloom,
> The fostered hyacinths spread their purple bloom.

And no shadow-lover but must delight (though once more a moral has to be avoided) in this picture of lambs on a May morning:

> they shun
> Pale twilight's lingering glooms, and in the sun
> Couch near their dams, with quiet satisfied:
> Or gambol—each with his shadow at his side,
> Varying its shape wherever he may run.
> As they from turf yet hoar with sleepy dew
> All turn, and court the shining and the green . . .

The phrases of this simile suggest a peculiar observation of Wordsworth, who dwells as no other English poet[1] has done upon the different aspects of landscape when seen looking toward or away from the sun, or at different times of the day. So in a picture of shadows at the opening of the *Excursion:*

> 'Twas summer, and the sun had mounted high;
> Southward the landscape indistinctly glared
> Through a pale steam; but all the northern downs,
> In clearest air ascending showed far off
> A surface dappled o'er with shadows flung
> From brooding clouds; shadows that lay in spots
> Determined and unmoved, with steady beams
> Of bright and pleasant sunshine interposed.

At the bursting out of the sun in the late afternoon, after a storm, the differing aspects of east and west are thus noticed, in the *Descriptive Sketches:*

> Eastward in long perspective glittering, shine
> The wood crowned cliffs that o'er the lake recline,
> Those lofty cliffs a hundred streams unfold,
> At once to pillars turned that flame with gold;
> Behind his sail the peasant shrinks, to shun
> The west, that burns as one dilated sun . . .

Such variations of light and shadow are particularly interesting in mountain scenery, and are most fre-

---

[1] This subject is interestingly treated in detail by such writers on landscape and the picturesque as Price, Gilpin and Repton; but it seems unlikely that Wordsworth derived any of his ideas from them, since he began as a boy to notice such effects. Their conclusions, too, while often excellent, are laboured; his touch is inspired.

quently used by the poet in that connexion. He notices
in the *Evening Walk* how

> in the south, the wan noon brooding still,
> Breath'd a pale steam around the glaring hill,
> And shades of deep embattled clouds were seen
> Spotting the northern cliffs with lights be-
> tween . . .

In the *Waggoner* he observes the dawn at Grasmere:

> While yet the valley is arrayed
> On this side with a sober shade;
> On that is prodigally bright—
> Crag, lawn, and wood—with rosy light.

In the *Guide* he tells how the sun, setting in summer,
is seen from the shore of "Winandermere, resting
among the summits of the loftiest mountains, some of
which will perhaps be half or wholly hidden by clouds,
or by the blaze of light which the orb diffuses around
it, and the surface of the lake will reflect before the
eye correspondent colours through every variety of
beauty, and through all degrees of splendour. In
the vale of Keswick, at the same period, the sun sets
over the humbler regions of the landscape, and showers
down upon *them* the radiance which at once veils and
glorifies,—sending forth meanwhile, broad streams of
rosy, crimson, purple, or golden light, towards the
grand mountains in the south and southeast, which,

thus illuminated, with all their projections and cavities, and with an intermixture of solemn shadows, are seen distinctly through a cool and clear atmosphere. Of course, there is a marked difference between the noon-tide appearance of these two opposite vales. The be-dimming haze that overspreads the south, and the clear atmosphere and determined shadows of the clouds in the north, at the same time of the day, are each seen in these several vales, with a contrast as striking."

The differing directions of its vales, which, roughly, radiate from a common centre, is one of the great advantages which Wordsworth discovered in the English Lakeland; a vast diversity of effects of light and shade being thus found within a small territory.

Similar contrast, though not of *mountain* light and shade, forms the substance of a passage on Grasmere churchyard, in the *Excursion:*

> when in changeful April fields are white
> With new-fallen snow, if from the sullen north
> Your walk conduct you hither, ere the sun
> Hath gained his noontide height, this churchyard, filled
> With mounds transversely lying side by side
> From east to west, before you will appear
> An unillumined, blank, and dreary plain . . .
> . . . Go forward, and look back;
> Look from the quarter whence the lord of light,
> Of life, and love and gladness doth dispense

> His beams; which, unexcluded in their fall,
> Upon the southern side of every grave
> Have gently exercised a melting power;
> *Then* will a vernal prospect greet your eye,
> All fresh and beautiful, and green and bright,
> Hopeful and cheerful . . .

(Here, of course, the sunbeams have done more than merely illumine the scene.)

The *Lines written while sailing in a Boat at Evening*, composed when Wordsworth was nineteen, have an early example of the effect:

> How richly glows the water's breast
> Before us, tinged with evening's hues,
> While facing thus the crimson west,
> The boat her silent course pursues;
> And see how dark the backward stream!
> A little moment past so smiling!

And *Stepping Westward* suggests it ideally—

> The dewy ground was dark and cold;
> Behind all gloomy to behold—

the travellers, "stepping westward," with "such a sky" to lead them on, felt moving into "that region bright" to be "a kind of heavenly destiny."

Wordsworth's interest in delicate modulations of light and shade led to several observations of the dif-

ferent quality of a view when seen from an enclosed
space. This may be a room, as when the Solitary of
the *Excursion* gazed

> Upon the landscape of the sunbright vale,
> Seen from the shady room in which we sate,
> In softened perspective—

or a cave; a scene is called most pleasant to him who
sees it from "the front of some huge cave," the rocky
ceiling of which casts a twilight of its own, an ample
shade; the watcher

> With sidelong eye looks out upon the scene,
> By power of that impending covert thrown
> To finer distance.

And how fair was the vision of the White Doe

> when it crossed the Maid
> Within some rocky cavern laid,
> The dark cave's portal gliding by,
> White as whitest cloud on high
> Floating through the azure sky.

So rich and beautiful is Wordsworth's treatment of
shadow and its play. Yet there is a mood, possibly his
highest mood, in which he is the poet of light, clear,
unspotted, and undimmed.

> Leave to the nightingale her shady wood,
> A privacy of glorious light is thine,

he cries to the skylark. Poems all characteristic, yet so different as the *Lines Written in March, Poor Susan,* the sonnet *It is a Beauteous Evening,* and that on Westminster Bridge, *Resolution and Independence,* the *Immortality Ode,* and the first part of the stanzas on Peele Castle, agree in being poems of light, and in owing to it a vital part of their being. We have seen how Wordsworth loved the moon in clouds, how he cited the clouded moon of *Paradise Lost,* and dreamed of

> Sweet Spenser, moving through his clouded heaven
> With the moon's beauty and the moon's soft pace;

yet the sonnet on Milton sounds perhaps the higher note—

> Pure as the naked heavens . . .

Minor effects of light interested Wordsworth; as he liked spots of colour, and points of light burning in darkness, so he enjoyed specks, flashes, and sparkles of brightness. The fourteenth Duddon sonnet speaks of

> A field or two of brighter green, or plot
> Of village-ground, that seemeth like a spot
> Of stationary sunshine.

A winter picture of Grasmere shows how

the birch-tree woods
Are hung with thousand, thousand diamond drops
Of melted hoar-frost, every tiny knot
In the bare twigs, each little budding-place
Cased with its several beads; what myriads these
Upon one tree, while all the distant grove
That rises to the summit of the steep,
Shows like a mountain built of silver light.

Dorothy Wordsworth's notes on a frosty day well paint what pleased both sister and brother: "We observed the lemon-coloured leaves of the birches, as the breeze turned them to the sun, sparkle, or rather flash, like diamonds, and the leafless purple twigs were tipped with globes of shining crystal." The poet writes of dew flashing like diamonds, the frost "with spangled tissue quaint," the faggots sparkling on the hearth, glittering vanes, sparkling light on stones, glistening flung on rocks, and diamond light whose "restless lustre" made his fancy restless as itself, when

the summer sun, declining, smote
A smooth rock wet with constant springs . . .
Sparkling from out a copse-clad bank that rose
Fronting our cottage.

Play of light on stones pleased him. There is the "votive stone" to the memory of the Swiss Captain-General, Aloys Reding, near the outlet of the Lake of Thun, where when the sun sinks

> all is dim, save this bright stone,
> Touched by his golden finger.

Wordsworth has stones "sparry and bright, rough scatterings of the hills": and he often remarks the beauty of wet stones, as that one "of the sea-beach," which when

> polished with nice care,
> Veins it discovers, exquisite and rare,
> Which for the loss of that moist gleam alone
> That tempted first to gather it, atone—.

There are also beds of streams floored with pebbles bright,

> Stones of all hues, gem emulous of gem,
> So vivid that they take from keenest sight
> The liquid veil that seeks not to hide them.[1]

It is significant that the word "glitter" is so frequent and such a favourite with Wordsworth. With its inflections, he uses it no less than 78 times. For him plainly it had none of the shallow, hard association we now feel in it, for when from Westminster Bridge he saw how London slept, and wore in touching ma-

---

[1] Colour in stones always interested Wordsworth. He speaks in the *Guide* (p. 116) of the great heaps of stones on the top of Scafell, "there left to be covered with never-dying lichens, which the clouds and dews nourish; and adorn with colours of vivid and exquisite beauty. Flowers, the most brilliant feathers, and even gems, scarcely surpass in colouring some of those masses of stone, which no human eye beholds, except the shepherd or traveller." . . .

jesty the beauty of the morning, her "ships, towers, domes, theatres, and temples" lay (he says) bright and *glittering* in the smokeless air. He has a skylark "glittering and twinkling near yon rosy cloud;" also "glittering laurels." Dorothy, too, made much use of this word.

It is interesting and helpful to trace these ways and idiosyncracies of Wordsworth. We do not feel that we really know our friends until we know their particular tastes, even their whims. These individual characteristics cannot be dissociated from the sum of the physical, intellectual, and moral nature of even a great poet; the nature which, joined with his own peculiar experience, makes his poetry his own and no other's.

We may leave Wordsworth's treatment of light and colour with a clearer impression of his individuality in the larger sense if we look for a moment at a characteristic piece of his work beside that of others.

Here are sunset images from three poets. From Shelley:

> In the golden lightning
> Of the sinking sun,
> O'er which clouds are brightening . . .

From Keats, two; first (to Apollo):

> When thy gold breath is misting in the west . . .

and then:

> When barred clouds bloom the soft-dying day
> And tinge the stubble-fields with rosy hue . . .

Now from Wordsworth:

> *"What, you are stepping westward?"*
> The dewy ground was dark and cold;
> Behind, all gloomy to behold;
> And stepping westward seemed to be
> A kind of *heavenly* destiny:
> I liked the greeting; 'twas a sound
> Of something without place or bound;
> And seemed to give me spiritual right
> To travel through that region bright.
>
> . . . while my eye
> Was fixed upon the glowing Sky,
> The echo of the voice enwrought
> A human sweetness with the thought
> Of travelling through the world that lay
> Before me in my endless way.

These glories of the closing day differ from one another as their poets differ. Each expresses something of the very being of its author. Whether or not Wordsworth could, he never did give in so few words the swift ethereal glory of Shelley's sunset west, or the fullness of colour with which Keats turned the west to gold, and "bloomed" the autumnal air and earth. The brooding concentrated romance of Keats, and the flight of Shelley, who floats and runs like his skylark among the elements to which he seems akin, wholly different as they are from each other, are also totally different from the imagination of Wordsworth, which, by a flash of illumination, links the sunset glow and the incident of a lonely evening walk with that "infinitude" in which is hidden man's "destiny," his "being's heart and home."

At his best the poet is the most individual; it is then, also, that his poetry most fully escapes analysis. For the sacred fire of poetry, kindling in the translucent urn of the poet's mind, reveals the form, the material, the markings, flaws, and texture of that which strives to contain it. But being infinite in itself, it cannot be contained, and forever escapes. We may describe the urn, and we may watch the light that irradiates it, but this light, pouring up into the region from which it came, transcends our definitions.

"Wordsworth's Seat" in the Wordsworth Garden at Cole Orton Hall

THE "IDIOT BOY"

Wordsworth to the end of his days could never understand why the poem of the *Idiot Boy,* which he had written with such a fervid delight, was not equally delightful to all his readers. The question is surely one of some interest. And even if much that is to be said has been said before, the bringing together of various scattered and rather fragmentary judgments may serve to create a clearer, more complete impression, and thus be not a mere vain repetition.

It will be well, then, before attempting any answer, to review some of the classical opinions of the piece. Hazlitt, on first hearing it read by Coleridge, "was not critically or sceptically inclined; I saw touches of truth and nature, and took the rest for granted;" but on the same occasion he felt in the *Thorn,* the *Mad Mother,* and *Complaint of a Poor Indian Woman* "the deeper power and pathos which have since been acknowledged." Dorothy Wordsworth, writing four years after the date of the poem, says: "I worked, and read the Lyrical Ballads, enchanted with the Idiot Boy." Southey, in the *Critical Review,* said it "resembles a Flemish picture in the worthlessness of its design, and excellence of its execution.". The *Analytical* (Dec. 1798), "warmly commends" the piece, and the *British*

Critic (Oct. 1798), considers it "animated by much interest, and told with singular felicity."[1]

Byron, in the youthful malice of his *English Bards and Scotch Reviewers* (1809), that "miserable record of misplaced anger and indiscriminate acrimony," as he afterwards called it, selected for the climax of his attack on Wordsworth,

> the tale of Betty Foy,
> The idiot mother of "an idiot boy;"
> A moon-struck, silly lad, who lost his way,
> And like his bard, confounded night with day;
> So close on each pathetic part he dwells,
> And each adventure so sublimely tells,
> That all who view the "idiot in his glory,"
> Conceive the bard the hero of the story.

The authors of the *Rejected Addresses* (published in 1812), preface their parody of Wordsworth,—*The Baby's Debut*—with these lines from the poet Cumberland:

> Thy lisping prattle and thy mincing gait,
> All thy false mimic fooleries I hate;
> For thou are Folly's counterfeit, and she
> Who is right foolish hath the better plea;
> Nature's true idiot I prefer to thee.

In 1833 the parodists confessed with feeling that "in no instance were we betrayed into greater injustice than

---

[1] Several of the criticisms above are taken from a reprint of the *Lyrical Ballads,* edited, with introduction and notes, by Thomas Hutchinson, Duckworth.

in the case of Mr. Wordsworth . . . we pounced upon his popular ballads, and exerted ourselves to push their simplicity into puerility and silliness."

Wordsworth, at the end of a letter to Coleridge, gives an amusing table of "harmonies of criticism," as he calls them, arranged by himself in a manner which proves him not incapable of a playful fun; and here, memorable circumstance! for once at least in his life, he is seen to smile at the expense of his own poetry. Our poem gets the following appreciations:

Idiot Boy	*Idiot Boy*
Mr. J. W. "A lady, a friend of mine, could talk of nothing else; this, of all the poems, her delight."	Mr. S. "Almost thrown by it into a fit of disgust! cannot read it!"

Wordsworth admits to "Christopher North," who had objected to the piece, that "this poem has, I know, frequently produced the same effect as it did upon you and your friends; but there are many also to whom it affords exquisite delight, and who, indeed, prefer it to any other of my poems." Coleridge called it "a fine poem," but made some definite criticisms, which will be better touched on later.

Amid this variety of opinion, it is on the whole, the best judges who best like the poem.

Of recent critics, Swinburne and Sir Walter Raleigh may suffice. The poet, enthusiast for Wordsworth though he was, called this and the *Thorn* "doleful examples of eccentricity in dullness." Sir Walter Raleigh observes that "the thing has some of the points of a fine poem, but it curvets and frisks so uncontrollably that it can hardly be recognised for what it is."

In our day, however, little is said of the piece; the critics, with the huge mass of Wordsworth's work before them from which to choose, have passed by to matters of greater importance. But now, in the hope of a little added light on the poet's mind, let us approach our question. And since most of us read the poem with imperfect sympathy, it will be better put in this form: Why was a composition which to the greater number, probably, of its readers seems to fail, and to fail ludicrously, so near to the heart of its maker?

Let us examine what he tells us himself about its making. The *Idiot Boy*, he explains, originated thus: "The last stanza—'The Cocks did crow to-whoo, to-whoo, and the sun did shine so cold'—was the foundation of the whole. The words were reported to me by my dear friend Thomas Poole; but I have since heard the same repeated of other Idiots." As to his feelings at the time of its composition, after saying that this long poem was composed extempore, and without corrections, in the groves of Alfoxden, he goes on, "I mention this in gratitude to those happy moments, for, in truth, I never wrote anything with so much glee." Not only did the words come to him rapidly, he felt a similar swiftness in the movement of the piece. A friend advised the insertion of an explanatory stanza: "but the narration in the poem is so rapid and impassioned, that I could not find a place in which to insert the stanza without checking the progress of it, and so leaving a deadness upon the feeling." (He did, however, in 1827, bring himself to strike out two particularly outrageous stanzas, the original third and fifth.) Again: "I wrote the poem with exceeding delight and pleasure, and whenever I read it, I read it with pleasure."

What were his poetic intentions in the *Idiot Boy?* In a letter to him, Christopher North objected, in connection with this piece, that nothing is a fit subject for poetry which does not please. Wordsworth replied, "Does not please whom?" and pointed out that "we err lamentably" if we suppose "people in our rank of life" to be fair representatives of the great mass of humanity. "And yet few ever consider books but with reference to their power of pleasing those persons and men of a higher rank; few descend lower, among cottages and fields, and among children. A man must have done this habitually before his judgment upon the "Idiot Boy" would be in any way decisive with me . . . You have given me praise for having reflected faithfully in my Poems the feelings of human nature. I would fain hope that I have done so. But a great Poet ought to do more than this; he ought, to a certain degree, to rectify men's feeling, to give them new compositions of feeling, to render their feelings more sane, pure, and permanent, in short, more consonant to Nature, that is, to eternal Nature, and the great moving Spirit of things. He ought to travel before men occasionally as well as at their sides."

Wordsworth wished, then, in this poem (or did he only think he wished?), to please the simple and untaught; as for refined persons who did not like it, he wished to "rectify" their taste by enlarging their sympathies. Unfortunately he neglects to say whether the simple did like it—history, also, has been too silent on this point—and it is to be feared that the recalcitrant of other classes have not yet fully appreciated how shining is the goal they have not reached.

In the same letter the poet says much in defence of the choice of an idiot as subject. His arguments are well enough, but we must notice, before looking at them, that Wordsworth betrays a partial realisation of the truth which, acted upon, would have made such argument scarcely necessary—that it was his choice of the word "idiot" which (as he says) "is a principal cause of . . . dislike to this particular poem. If there had been any such word in our language, to which we had attached passion, as lack-wit, half-wit, witless, etc., I should certainly have employed it in preference; but there is no such word." If he could neither find nor coin such a word—and his suggested substitutes are

not happy—he should at least have avoided the one he
did use, which is undoubtedly offensive and a stumb-
ling-block to readers, though it is clear that Wordsworth himself minded it not a whit. Sir Walter Raleigh
even concludes, from Wordsworth's sentence, that he
attached passion to the very name "Idiot." While this
conclusion does not seem to follow necessarily from
the phrase "any"—not "any *other*"—"such word in our
language," Wordsworth really seems to have used with
gusto that repeated rhyme-ending of "idiot-boy."

To turn to the poet's argument. He continues, that
the disgust associated with idiots by many persons
arises in great measure from "false delicacy" and "a
certain want of comprehensiveness of thinking and
feeling;" while the humbler classes, "seeing frequently
among their neighbours such objects, easily forget
whatever there is of natural disgust about them, and
have therefore a sane state, so that without pain or
suffering they perform their duties toward them." His
own idiot, however, he carefully explains (thus showing a sense of some weakness in his general principle)
"the 'Boy' whom I had in my mind, was by no means
disgusting in his appearance, quite the contrary." But
this explanation he did not make in the poem (the
stanza for the insertion of which he could not check the
impassioned rush of the narrative was to have done
this important work) ; and it is on this point that Coleridge made one of his two criticisms,—"the only plausi-

ble objection which I have heard to that fine poem."
The author, he says, was not careful to preclude ordinary unpleasant images of idiocy, "which yet it was by
no means his intention to represent. He has even by
the burr, burr, burr, uncounteracted by any preceding
description of the boy's beauty, assisted in recalling
them."

But the vital part of Wordsworth's argument, that
in which we may see his deeper mind, the "very pulse
of the machine," is this:

> I have often applied to idiots, in my own mind,
> the sublime expression of Scripture, that "their
> life is hidden with God." They are worshipped,
> probably from a feeling of this sort, in several
> parts of the East. Among the Alps, where they
> are numerous, they are considered, I believe, as
> a blessing to the family to which they belong. I
> have, indeed, often looked upon the conduct of
> fathers and mothers of the lower classes of so-
> ciety toward idiots as the great triumph of the
> human heart. It is there that we see the strength,
> grandeur, and disinterestedness of love; nor have
> I ever been able to contemplate an object that
> calls out so many excellent and virtuous senti-
> ments without finding it hallowed thereby, and
> having something in me which bears down before
> it, like a deluge, every feeble sensation of disgust
> and aversion.

However, intolerable we of the present age may find
it that idiots should, as a matter of course, be "numer-

ous" in any place, the social reformer is to be pitied who is not able also to feel as Wordsworth felt. The unmistakable strength of his feeling may teach us something of the origin of the poem.

Maternal love was one of the great primal emotions over which the mind of Wordsworth was wont to brood. Into this poem enters that love in the form which he felt to be so peculiarly moving. And it must always be remembered that the boy who is the object of this affection is a *young* child,—"a little idle sauntering thing," his mother in her vexation calls him. We know how Wordsworth saw in the actions and impressions of the simple, unspoiled child, a far-brought celestial wisdom,—that blest vision "which we are toiling all our lives to find." But here, joined to the simplicity of childhood, is the further simplicity of the "natural," of him whose "life is hid with God;" a soul thus doubly open, as Wordsworth believed, to the influence of Nature, and what lies beyond Nature.

Thus is the Boy a hero peculiarly to Wordsworth's mind, or to one side of his mind. It is the "pure fool," potent by his utter failure in the wisdom of this world.

Another important consideration is the setting of the piece, a blue moonlight night; for this was one especially dear to the poet. The moon pervades the story. It is

a clear March night;
The moon is up,—the sky is blue.

193

"As sure as there's a moon in heaven" Betty keeps ex-
claiming; and Johnny's adventure ends when

> the moon was setting on the hill,
> So pale you scarcely looked at her,

And added to the moonlight there is, in the scene of
adventure, that solitary silence, accentuated by the
cries of owls, which Wordsworth always found so rich
in imaginative suggestion.

> The owlet, in the moonlight air,
> Shouts from nobody knows where . . .
> With the owls began my song,
> And with the owls must end.

There are two stanzas full of the spirit of night, when
Betty goes abroad to seek her boy.

> She listens, but she cannot hear
> The foot of horse, the voice of man;
> The streams with softest sounds are flowing,
> The grass you almost hear it growing,
> You hear it now, if e'er you can.
> The owlets through the long blue night
> Are shouting to each other still:
> Fond lovers! not yet quite hob-nob,
> They lengthen out the tremulous sob
> That echoes far from hill to hill.

Hero and situation, then, are potentially rich in poetic
interest. Here is a complete equipment, too, for a sym-

bolic presentment of "the soul's adventure,"—the helpless, untried being sent suddenly forth, with a beast it knows not how to manage, on a mission it can never fully comprehend, into a bewildering world of changing lights and shadows, and mysterious sounds. It is easy to imagine what charming fairy-tales more recent poets might concoct of it; but Wordsworth was made of sterner stuff.

The quest of this Parsifal is quite in keeping; it is one of healing; on this point, however, it is not advisable to insist. The doctor was not fetched, but as the patient made a perfect recovery without him, we need have no regrets. Wordsworth himself cared nothing for the ostensible mission. It has the slightest connexion with the real adventure, which, for mother and son, is, in one word, joy. Our "natural" spent the night in joy, in a glory of glee. And the elements of this joy are, for the child, freedom, power, responsibility, accorded to one never before held worthy of them; for the mother, all these echoing along the tender nerves of maternal' pride.

We read of the boy that when the pony moved its legs,

> For joy he cannot hold the bridle,
> For joy his head and heels are idle,
> He's idle all for very joy . . .

and

> His heart it was so full of glee . . .
> He quite forgot his holly whip.

And all his skill in horsemanship:
Oh! happy, happy, happy, John.

The delightful things the child might have done in his
hours of solitary wandering the poet suggests, but our
fancy is tied down to none of them. The deeds and
thoughts of that night remain a mystery.

The adventure is, on the whole, also one of joy to
the mother. When her son departs,

> her face with joy o'erflows
> Proud of herself and proud of him . . . ;

she

> Could lend out of that moment's store
> Five years of happiness or more
> To any that might need it.

And when after the interval of anxiety and troubled
search, she finds "him whom she loves," "she screams
—she cannot move for joy," while Johnny

> laughs aloud;
> Whether in cunning or in joy
> I cannot tell; but while he laughs,
> Betty a drunken pleasure quaffs . . .

She is "almost stifled with her bliss"—

> She's happy here, is happy there,
> She is uneasy everywhere;
> Her limbs are all alive with joy.

Old Susan too appearing, "as if by magic cured,"—

> Oh me! it was a merry meeting
> As ever was in Christendom,

cries the poet, in a final burst.

So ends the Joyous Quest after its interlude of woe and fear, in a perfection of triumph possible only to the simple-hearted. The human emotions of the poem are all those workings of wholly unsophisticated natures in which Wordsworth found one of his deepest interests.

It was an interest which some of his most important friends were unable fully to share. John Wilson wrote that "the affection of Betty Foy has nothing in it to excite interest . . . The excessive fondness of the mother disgusts us . . . to me it appears almost unnatural that a person in a state of complete idiotism should excite the warmest feelings of attachment in the breast even of his mother." Christopher North evidently knew not the heart of woman. Coleridge's second definite criticism was also directed at the folly of the mother, which, he says, appears "rather a laughable burlesque on the blindness of anile dotage, than an analytic display of maternal affection in its ordinary workings." "An analytic display" was certainly not what Wordsworth sought, and by this chill phrase Coleridge shows himself, here, out of harmony with the spirit of the poem. To the creator of *Christabel* and the *Mariner* the peasant raptures of Betty Foy might indeed, as a moonlight rhapsody, offer little beyond extravagance of degree and crudity of expression.

The underlying conception, then, of the adventure, as well as of the hero and the background, is truly poetic; and in all these felicitious elements we may find the first answer as to Wordsworth's delight in the piece. They were exactly suited to some of his most characteristic powers. The materials of the poem might well have been wrought into a thing of beauty, and a beauty most Wordsworthian.

Why, then, did he make of them a thing which makes readers laugh at it, or turn away bored or impatient, instead of feeling his own exquisite pleasure?

The reason is found in the mood in which Wordsworth wrote. The conception of this poem and the mood is which it was written are two surprisingly distinct things.

Dowden said of the *Idiot Boy:* "At rare times in his poetry Wordsworth shows an inclination for frolic; it is the frolic of good spirits in one habitually grave, and he cannot caper lightly and gracefully." And Sir Walter Raleigh regards "the garrulous and vain repetitions" of this piece as "the effervescence of the wildest high spirits: the narrative, like the mother of the idiot, 'cannot move for joy;' and the diction, like her son, is 'idle all for very joy'." But while the "glee" in which the poet wrote seems indeed high spirits, surely it is also something more. It is a strong welling-up of the

humour in which he is sometimes wrongly thought to
be entirely wanting.

The narrative is unquestionably treated in a spirit of
humour; it almost arrives at being funny in the pony,
who is

> a horse that thinks,
> Yet for his life he cannot tell
> What he has got upon his back,

and in the awakened Doctor who shows at the casement

> His glimmering eyes that peep and doze,

"while one hand rubs his old night-cap," and in his re-
ply to Betty's inquiry for her boy, who's "not so wise
as some folks be"—

> "The devil take his wisdom!" said
> The Doctor, looking somewhat grim,
> "What, Woman! should I know of him?"
> And, grumbling, he went back to bed.

Humour in Wordsworth was infrequent and peculiar. It was ungenial; it did not, like the finest humour,
draw warmth and brightness from the sympathetic
kindling of others to the same perceptions. Wordsworth's was self-sufficient; there is in it something of
the inhuman arrogance with De Qincy felt in the
poet's social behavior. He is too completely carried

away by his amusement to make us share it. His laughter sounds harsh and unseemly, because he is so lost in the enjoyment of it that he cares not whether it echoes in other hearts. "Everything is tedious when one does not read with the feelings of the author," he says of this and other poems; but we have a right to complain when the author does not take the trouble to awaken those feelings. It is only by effort, by trying to trace the course of the poet's mirth, that one may here come to a degree of sympathy with it.

One comes thus also to a realisation that Wordsworth's sense of humour was only elementary. His laughter, like a boy's is excited, and excited unduly, by the feebly funny; while on the other hand the really amusing passes over his head. The situations and story of the *Idiot Boy* have excellent possibilities of humour. From this point of view, the climax of the poem is this: that when Betty has herself performed the journey on which she had sent her son, she should reach the Doctor's door, and even talk with him, without its ever occurring to her that old Susan was still supposed to be in that dire need of his assistance which had made the errand necessary. But Wordsworth makes nothing of this; he merely says, "This piteous news" (of Johnny's non-appearance),

> it so much shocked her,
> She quite forgot to send the Doctor
> To comfort poor old Susan Gale.

Rhyme and rhetoric alike fail him; and throughout the poem he does not really develop the humour of the situations, but continues to gloat over his own amusement.

And this amusement arose, we know, from the words of an idiot who mistook the owls for cocks and the moon for sun; a confusion which so struck Wordsworth's sense of humour as to induce a mood of almost uproarious mirth which persisted throughout the ninety stanzas of this poem. But there is really nothing so extremely funny in the confusion. In intelligent people it would usually arouse at most a passing ripple of merriment. Dowden said truly that Wordsworth "teaches us many things, but he does not teach us how to laugh wisely and kindly." For if we are left by this poem in that state of enlarged sympathies desired by the poet, it is rather in spite of his long, loud laughter than because of it.

In Wordsworth's appearance Hazlitt noted "a convulsive inclination to laughter, a good deal at variance with the solemn, stately expression of the rest of the face." This description was quoted by Dowden in significant connexion with the *Idiot Boy*, whose "conception" and "mood" we find to be in keys so different.

"I never wrote anything with so much glee." It is not that humour, at this ecstatic pitch, need be wholly inconsistent with the serious imaginative qualities of the poem; but that the full torrent of it, its "waves that own no curbing hand," quite overwhelm them, and sweep them on with such force that they are lost to view.

Here, then, is part of the secret of the rush and swiftness which Wordsworth (and surely Wordsworth alone!) felt in the piece. It was to him, as well as much besides, a huge joke, and everyone knows too well how a joke which to the relater rushes in a dazzle of interest to its conclusion, may be of all things most slow and dragging to a listener.

And here, again, is a second answer, but this time a perfectly obvious answer, to the question of Wordsworth's unshared delight in the poem. It was mainly because he had immensely enjoyed writing what he found so richly amusing that he ever after associated this delight with the poem, and could not see why his readers missed it.

The incongruity which Hazlit saw in Wordsworth's face, and which can be discerned in this poem, may teach us afresh that Wordsworth, though his too-early aging mind hid itself in platitudes and moralisings, was, in his poetic season, a being in whom enormous forces met, forces sometimes unrestrained and "convulsive." As in all great poets, there was in him the Titan, and the Titan, whether in his mirth or his majesty, is not always in good taste or quite intelligible to mankind in general. The Titan is at work in the *Idiot Boy*, and to find the piece merely insipid, trivial, or absurd, is to miss an instructive opportunity.

Residence of Mr. Wordsworth
Rydal Mount. Sept: 1844

SKETCH OF RYDAL MOUNT BY HENRY INMAN

"THE HAPPIEST-LOOKING HOMES OF MEN"

Wordsworth's conception of home is unique in poetry. His contemporaries scarcely touch the idea. It is a subject no more to be looked for in Byron than the famous "leg of mutton in a gin-shop." Keats, if he had lived, and lived happily, might have included it in his range with other human interests; as it was, he got as far as

> Sit thee by the ingle when
> The sear faggot blazes bright,
> Spirit of a winter's night . . .

Shelley remained forever a wild thing, inhabiting the whole of earth and sea and sky. It is worth noting that of four almost contemporaneous poems on the skylark, Wordsworth's two and Hogg's all bring in the touching note of the bird's return from the sky to its nest and home; Shelley's lark alone seems to soar eternally at heaven's gate.

Coleridge, in his beautiful *Frost at Midnight*, comes very close to Wordsworth's conception. It is a poem which admits us into the spirit of Coleridge, and into that part of his spirit which made him the intimate of William Wordsworth. But as regards this subject, it does little more than suggest ideas which his friend was so fully to develop. Crabbe, like Wordsworth, has vivid pictures of cottage homes; but in a part of England so different from his, he saw in them the wretchedness of the poor, not the beauty possible to lowly dwellings.

Burns, indeed, in the *Cotter's Saturday Night*, achieved a classic of home. But it is the home of family life, pure and simple. Its joys, affections, and interests are so strictly domestic, so self-contained, that its atmosphere would be close and stifling but for the poem's opening out into Burn's vision of the national life as founded on the peasant home and its virtues.

Such an atmosphere never oppresses in Wordsworth; for a different reason. Pious he was, domesticated he was; but in spite of these desolating traits, even in the most uninspired period of his advancing years the home in his poetry was ventilated by one constant living breath which enters not at all into the poem of Burns. This breath, this freshening wave out of the universal atmosphere, is the breath of Nature.

The ideal home for Charles and Mary Lamb was a fireside in London, and the company of each other, their books, and their friends. William and Dorothy Wordsworth, even with each other, could not have been truly happy under the "black sky," "alone in the multitude," of the city whose walls are "barricaded with sorrow." It is impossible to imagine them permanently there; their personalities dissolve; they cease to be themselves.

The one true home for Wordsworth was a dwelling, whether fine or humble, in close relation with Nature.

For the nearness of Nature was an essential part of his idea of home; and it is the distinguishing characteristic of that idea in his poetry. The dwelling, associated in habit and memory with the grounds or fields, woods or mountains among which it stands, becomes with them an object of love and delight. It is thus for Wordsworth not only, as with Burns, the scene of family life, but a thing living also in the life of Nature; so long, so fully, sharing in her influences of skies and seasons and growth, as to seem actually one of her works and part of her being.

Wordsworth's sense of this is best shown when he writes of the cottage,—the scene of how many of his poems. Here was the favourite theatre of his studies of human life and of the deep, silent joys and griefs of the people he understood, though they never, it seems, understood him. Among the Lakeland cottages he passed his school-boy days; in such a cottage were spent, with his wonderful sister, those years of his young manhood when "imagination and taste" had been restored in him to more than their original power. Here he conversed with Coleridge; here he brought his young wife, and here children were born to him. The lover of Wordsworth can never dissociate the poetry written at this time from Dove Cottage, and from the life there as recorded by Dorothy Wordsworth.

Before beginning to look at his treatment of the cot-

tage-home, it is well to observe that Wordsworth did
not idealise it.

> Bleak and bare
> They found the cottage, their allotted home;
> Naked without, and rude within,

he writes. His own chimneys smoked, much to his dis-
comfort; and his sister once records: "W. did not sleep
from the rain coming into his room." At a later time
she "cannot but admire the fortitude with which he
has laboured on in that room, common to all the family,
to all visitors, and where the children frequently play
beside him." The cottage where dwelt the Solitary of
Blea Tarn

> had almost a forbidding nakedness;
> Less fair, I grant, even painfully less fair
> Than it appeared when from the beetling rock
> We had looked down upon it . . .

Its small apartment was "dark and low." Wordsworth's
Admonition, "intended more particularly for the peru-
sal of those who may have happened to be enamoured
of some beautiful Place of Retreat, in the Country of
Lakes," warns those whom some "lovely Cottage in the
guardian nook" has stirred deeply, not to covet the un-
suitable abode:

> Think what the home must be if it were thine,
> Even thine, though few thy wants! Roof,
> window, door,

206

The very flowers are sacred to the Poor,
The roses to the porch which they entwine:
Yea, all, that now enchants thee, from the day
On which it should be touched, would melt away.

The old Dalesman's cottage is as close to nature as any dwelling in which civilised man can, out of the tropics, live in reasonable comfort. Close to the ground, low-walled, and floored with flag-stones, it can yet be kept warm and dry and clean. In its position, as well as in materials, and construction, it is the natural outgrowth of its surroundings. The site of the old cottages, the *Guide to the Lakes* points out, was determined by the formation of the vales—"the several rocks and hills . . . rising up like islands from the level area of the vale" being chosen for dwelling-sites.

> Where none of these are found, and the inclination of the ground is not sufficiently rapid to carry off the water (as in the higher part of Langdale, for instance), the houses are not sprinkled over the middle of the vales, but confined to their sides, being placed merely so far up the mountain as to be protected from the floods. But where these rocks and hills have been scattered over the plain of the vale (as in Grasmere, Donnerdale, Eskdale, etc.), the beauty which they give to the scene is much heightened by a single cottage, or cluster of cottages, that will be almost always found under them or upon their sides; dryness and shelter having tempted the Dalesmen to fix their habitation there.

"Nature is thus responsible for the position of the cottages scattered over the valleys, and under the hillsides, and on the rocks;" she is also the artist who has shaped and coloured them. "The dwelling-houses and contiguous outhouse, are, in many instances, of the colour of the native rock; but frequently the Dwelling or Fire-house, as it is ordinarily called, has been distinguished from the barn or byre by rough-cast and whitewash, which, as the inhabitants are not hasty in renewing it, in a few years acquires, by the influence of weather, a tint at once sober and variegated." Passing from father to son, the houses have been changed according to the needs of the successive occupants.

> so that these humble dwellings remind the contemplative spectator of a production of Nature, and may (using a strong expression) rather be said to have grown than to have been erected;—to have risen, by an instinct of their own, out of the native rock—so little is there in them of formality, such is their wildness and beauty. Among the numerous recesses and projections in the walls, and in the different stages of the roofs, are seen bold and harmonious effects of contrasted sunshine and shadow.

"The strong winds which sweep down the valleys" caused many of these cottages to be furnished with substantial porches.

and such as have not this defence, are seldom un-
provided with a projection of two large slates
over their thresholds. Nor will the singular
beauty of the chimneys escape the eye of the
attentive traveler. Sometimes a low chimney,
almost upon a level with the roof, is overlaid with
a slate, supported upon four slender pillars, to
prevent the wind from drawing the smoke down
the chimney. Others are of a quadrangular
shape, rising one or two feet above the roof,
which low square is often surmounted by a tall
cylinder, giving to the cottage chimney the most
beautiful shape in which it is ever seen. Nor
will it be too fanciful or refined to remark that
there is a pleasing harmony between a tall chimney of this circular form, and the living column
of smoke, ascending from it through the still air.[1]

"These dwellings," the poet continues,

mostly built . . . of rough unhewn stone, are
roofed with slates, which were rudely taken from
the quarry before the present art of splitting
them was understood, and are, therefore, rough
and uneven in their surface, so that both the
coverings and sides of the houses have furnished

[1] "Wudsworth was a great un' for chimleys, had summut to say
in the making of a deal of 'em hereabout. There was most all the
chimleys Rydal way built after his mind. I 'member he and the Doctor
(Mr. Arnold) had great arguments about the chimleys time we was
building Foxhow, Wudsworth sed he liked a bit of colour in 'em. And
that the chimley coigns should be natural headed and natural bedded, a
little red and a little yallar. For there is a bit of colour in the quarry
stone up Easedale way. And he'ed a great fancy an aw for chimleys
square up hauf way, and round the t'other. And so we built 'em that
how." (From *Wordsworthiana; Reminiscences of Wordsworth*, by H.
B. Rawnsley: quoted in E. de Selincourt's edition of the *Guide to the
Lakes*, p. 187.)

places of rest for the seeds of lichens, mosses, ferns, and flowers. Hence buildings, which in their very form call to mind the processes of Nature, do thus, clothed in part with a vegetable garb, appear to be received into the bosom of the living principle of things, as it acts and exists among the woods and fields; and by their colour and their shape, affectingly direct the thoughts to that tranquil course of Nature and simplicity, along which the humble-minded inhabitants have, through so many generations, been led.[1]

The close relation between the cottage and its natural surroundings Wordsworth notices in such brief phrases as "the grey cottage by the stream," or "cottage shaded by woody crags." Of fuller descriptions there are several besides that of the *Guide*. There is the mountain cottage, a

> house of stones collected on the spot,
> By rude hands built, with rocky knolls in front,
> Backed also by a ledge of rock, whose crest
> Of birch-trees waves over the chimney-tops;
> A rough abode—in colour, shape and size

---

[1] John Wilson has interesting observations on these cottages. "Many of the Westmoreland cottages," he says, "would seem, to an ignorant observer, to have been originally built on a model conceived by the finest poetical genius. In the first place, they are almost always built precisely where they ought to be, had the builder's prime object been to beautify the dale . . . To feel the full force of the peculiar beauty of these antique tenements, you must understand their domestic economy. If ignorant of that, you can have no conception of the meaning of any one thing you see—roofs, eaves, chimneys, beams, props, doors, hovels, and sheds and hanging staircase, being all huddled together, as you think, in unintelligible confusion; whereas they are all precisely where they ought to be, and have had their colours painted, forms shaped, and places allotted by wind and weather, and the perpetually but pleasantly felt necessities of the natural condition of mountaineers." See the *Stroll to Grasmere*, in the *Recreations of Christopher North*, for details too full for quotation.

such as might in times of Border war have been contrived to elude the plunderer's eye.
Wordsworth has one seashore cottage in Devon—

> a low cottage in a sunny bay,
> Where the salt sea innocuously breaks,
> And the sea breeze as innocently breathes,
> A sheltered hold in a soft clime . . .

There is the cottage on the mountain-ridge, visited by the Wanderer and his companions, in Book VI of the *Excursion;* not seeming distinguished from the rudest habitations—

> Ye might think
> That it had sprung self-raised from earth, or grown
> Out of the living rock, to be adorned
> By nature only; but if thither led
> Ye would discover, then, a studious work
> Of many fancies, prompting many hands.

This uniting of its wild original character with the careful and loving work of man is one of the outstanding features of the cottage as seen by Wordsworth. The passage just quoted goes on—

> Brought from the woods the honeysuckle twines
> Around the porch, and seems, in that trim place
> A plant no longer wild; the cultured rose
> There blossoms, strong in health, and will be soon

Roof-high; the wild pink crowns the garden-wall,
And with the flowers are intermingled stones
Sparry and bright, rough scatterings of the
hills . . .

The mountain-cottage backed by the ledge of rock
has no such adornments ascribed to it, but does not lack
its own humanised beauty:

High on the breast of yon dark mountain, dark
With stony barrenness.

is seen a shining speck, that might be deemed a sleeping
sunbeam—

But 'tis a plot of cultivated ground,
Cut off, an island in the dusky waste,
And that attractive brightness is its own.

Thus in this wildest of spots the tilled green fields
about the cottage tell of the labour of man.

The Devon cottage, indebted to milder airs as well as
to cherishing hands, has its "unendangered myrtle,"
which, with holly and yew, promise to "endear the
hours of winter, and protect that pleasant place." The
dwelling of the Solitary at Blea Tarn had its human
charm of setting, the "plot of green sward," smooth
and commodious" for the pacing of the philosophic
friends. The Hawkshead homes of his school-days
were endeared to Wordsworth by their surroundings:

> Can I forget you, being as you were
> So beautiful among the pleasant fields
> In which ye stood?

In the *Memoir of Wordsworth* we read that J. T.
Coleridge and the poet walked towards Kirkstone by
Troutbeck, "passing by many interesting cots, barns,
and farm-houses, where W. had constantly something
to point out in the architecture, or the fringes of moss,
ferns, etc., on the roof or walls."

The cottage home with Wordsworth is close to
Nature not only by place and structure, but often by
its solitariness. He loved his own home especially for
its remoteness and inaccessibility. Coming even as a
"roving school-boy" to the verge of the vale of Grasmere on a golden summer holiday.

> with a sudden influx overpowered
> At sight of this seclusion, he forgot
> His haste . . .

and "sighed to live there." When that wish was ful-
filled in manhood, he cries

Embrace me then, ye Hills, and close me in—

and he sees the vale to be "pleased" with its

> church and cottages of mountain stone
> Clustered like stars, some few, but single most,
> And lurking dimly in their shy retreats,
> Or glancing at each other cheerful looks
> Like separated stars with clouds between.

The country he loved was a land of fields and habitations,

> seemingly preserved
> From all intrusion of the restless world
> By rocks impassable and mountains huge.

And "the genius of our hills," continues the poet, seems

> by these stupendous barriers cast
> Round his domain, desirous not alone
> To keep his own, but also to exclude
> All other progeny.

It is the solitary or single cottage of which Wordsworth oftenest and most feelingly writes. "Lucy's cot" was among "the untrodden ways;" it was "a single small cottage, a nest like a dove's" that swam visionary before the eyes and heart of Poor Susan; Michael's cottage, "The Evening Star,"

> on a plot of rising ground
> Stood single, with large prospect.

At Blea Tarn was

> One bare dwelling; one abode, no more!

The Priest's cottage in the *Excursion* was hidden and secluded. "A single mountain cottage"—"this one cottage in the lonely dale"—"solitary hut"—"the one cottage in the lonely dell"—"the Shepherd and his

Cot . . . privileged Inmate of deep solitude"—"deep
Valley, with thy one rude House"—such pictures are
familiar to Wordsworth's readers.

It is this very isolation which often brings the cottage
home into closest union with Nature. How rich to
Wordsworth's mind was the solitude of such a home
appears in the joy he felt in the situation of the Blea
Tarn cottage:

> a little lowly vale,
> A lowly vale, and yet uplifted high
> Among the mountains; even as if the spot
> Had been from eldest time by wish of theirs
> So placed, to be shut off from all the world!
> Urn-like it was in shape, deep as an urn;
> With rocks encompassed, save that to the south
> Was one small opening, where a heath-clad ridge
> Supplied a boundary less abrupt and close;
> A quiet treeless nook, with two green fields,
> A liquid pool that glittered in the sun,
> And one bare dwelling; one abode, no more!
> . . . full many a spot
> Of hidden beauty have I chanced to espy
> Among the mountains; never one like this;
> So lonesome. and so perfectly secure . . .
> In rugged arms how safely does it lie,
> How tenderly protected . . .
> To the still influx of the morning light
> Open, and day's pure cheerfulness, but veiled
> From human observation, as if yet
> Primeval forests wrapped [it] round with dark
> Impenetrable shade . . .

The security of the spot, protected by the wildness of Nature, is one reason for the poet's deep delight in it; another is its peace. It is

> By Nature destined from the birth of things
> For quietness profound.

It seems

> Like the fixed centre of a troubled world.

About it

> far and near
> We have an image of the pristine earth,
> The planet in its nakedness: were this
> Man's only dwelling, sole appointed seat,
> First, last and single, in the breathing world,
> It could not be more quiet; peace is here,
> Or nowhere.

A third and very real charm to the poet lay in such a dwelling's independence of the world without. The "rude House" of Blea Tarn had its small lot of "life-supporting fields."

> It seemed the home of poverty and toil,
> Though not of want; the little fields, made green
> By husbandry of many thrifty years,
> Paid cheerful tribute to the moorland house.

The spot was

Not melancholy—no, for it is green,
And bright, and fertile, furnished in itself
With the few needful things that life requires.

At Chatsworth, he contrasts the mansion and domain with

house or home in many a craggy rent
Of the wild Peak; where new-born waters glide
Through fields whose thrifty occupants abide
As in a dear and chosen banishment,
With every semblance of entire content,
So kind is simple Nature, fairly tried!

Of Grasmere Wordsworth cries

What want we? Have we not perpetual streams,
Warm woods and sunny hills, and fresh green
    fields,
And mountains not less green, and flocks and
    herds,
And thickets full of songsters, and the voice
Of lordly birds, an unexpected sound
Heard now and then from morn to latest eve,
Admonishing the man who walks below
Of solitude and silence in the sky?

Thus are the things needful to man's bodily life glorified for the poet by "unexpected" calls to his spirit from the infinite mystery of nature.

Wordsworth delighted in the thrift and care which, seizing upon every possible opportunity, made self-sustaining, pleasing homes of these poor and lonely dwellings. "While wandering on foot" (he writes), "through the fertile valleys and over the moorlands of the Apennine that divides Yorkshire from Lancashire, I used to be delighted with observing the number of substantial cottages that had sprung up on every side, each having its little plot of fertile ground, won from the surrounding waste. A bright warm fire, if needed, was always to be found in these dwellings. The father was at the loom, the children looked healthy and happy."

The mountain priest's dwelling, at first so "naked without and rude within," "shadeless and shelterless," not only sufficed for the needs of its inmates, "plentifully fed, though simply" from the household farm, with "timely treat of fish or fowl," but gradually, by thrift and fond diligence, was "trimmed and brightened." The poet details the shutters which "weather-fended," "repelled the storm and deadened its loud roar;" the snow-white curtains; the mats woven of mountain plants; the "fair carpet," woven of homespun wool, but "tinctured daintily with florid hues," to cover, on festal days, the stone-flagged floor; as well as the outside planting which kept

> The once-bare cottage on the mountain-side
> Screened from assault of every bitter blast;
> While the dark shadows of the summer leaves
> Danced in the breeze, chequering its mossy roof.

That those who live close to Nature may draw from her all that they need for body as well as mind was a belief that Wordsworth held, whose evidence he loved to detail. Thus he dwelt with ever-fresh pleasure on the surroundings of the cottage, and the circumstances of its life. Nothing can show this better than a passage from the *Guide to the Lakes,* which continues the account of the Dalesmen's cottage previously given.

> Add the little garden with its shed for bee-hives, its small bed of pot-herbs, and its borders and patches of flowers for Sunday posies, with sometimes a choice few too much prized to be plucked; an orchard of proportioned size; a cheese-press, often supported by some tree near the door; a cluster of embowering sycamores for summer shade; with a tall fir, through which the winds sing when other trees are leafless; the little rill or household spout murmuring in all seasons; combine these incidents and images together, and you have the representative idea of a mountain cottage in this country . . .

Into the cottage life enter the lives of the household or farm-yard creatures; "the bees around their range of sheltered hives;" "the cackling hen, the tender chicken brood;" the honest sheepdog; sheep and their lambs; the "wild birds that gather" round the porch; the red-breast that enters the house, or "ruffled up by winter's cold" "feeds at your hand;" the wren, building in a box hung from the casement—such are the creatures that Wordsworth associates with the cottage life as part of its interest and its being, another link with the world of Nature. The kitten playing with falling leaves, Peter Bell's suffering ass, the dog of *Fidelity* with its "love sublime," or the Curate's, which had "grown grey" with him, and after his death lived in "sadness no indulgence could prevent," or Barbara Lewthwaite's lamb, with its mother's heart working within it—such animals Wordsworth's imagination lifts from domesticated dullness into as high a world as the wild birds, whose life we can all see to be poetic.

With a similar light of imagination he can touch the objects connected with the habits of daily life in the cottage home, because they are close to Nature. The well under shading elms, the household rill, the porch of stones with its low bench, the cottage-lattice through which the moon softly peeps, the tall circular chimney "in pleasing harmony with its living column of smoke," all meant to the poet more than meets the common eye. A lantern held by a poor old woman becomes a memorable sight, because it is on a solitary and "aery height" that she stands holding it; and because its "unwearied signal, kenned afar," appearing "high in the gloom," will guide her husband home. This light appears

Not like a dancing meteor, but in line
Of never-varying motion, to and fro.

Human constancy, and tried affection in the solitude of Nature—these are the inward meaning of home to Wordsworth, and with such meaning this lantern shone for him. Another home light, undying in poetry, though in the sad story it failed, is that of Michael's cottage, which was "so regular and so far seen" as to give the house its name, The Evening Star.

Cottage life centres about the fireside. Wordsworth has sufficiently recorded his delight in his own hearth, which needed not the seasoning of "personal talk":—

Better than such discourse doth silence long,
Long, barren silence square with my desire;
To sit without emotion, hope, or aim,
In the loved presence of my cottage fire,
And listen to the flapping of the flame,
Or kettle whispering its faint undersong.

"Beside the glimmering fire . . . the cricket chirped, the house-dog dozed," in one cottage, or hut, giving comfort to a fugitive. For another worn wanderer a cottage-fire's

genial warmth seemed met
By a faint shining from the heart, a gleam
Of comfort, spread over his pallid face.

Such were the "plain comforts" of the cottage; a "genial hearth" where one might sit "by his fire, a child upon his knee;" a "blazing fire," a "cleanly hearth." Beside this fire, Wordsworth liked to hear the whir of the spinning-wheel—

> Soft as a Dorhawk's to the distant ear,
> When twilight shades darken the mountain head,

or

> Making the cottage through the silent hours
> Murmur as with the sound of summer flies.

His Lucy turned her wheel beside an English fire; he wrote a song to accompany the "pleasant labour" of the spinner, and deplored its passing:

> Grief, thou hast lost an ever-ready friend
> Now that the cottage spinning-wheel is mute.

"A kind influence to compose," in care, or love, or joy's excess, was this "venerable Art torn from the poor." And a mountain cottage charms most, he thinks, when "the gloom of night is falling," and through "the blazing window" is seen the eldest daughter at her wheel,

> Spinning amain, as if to overtake
> The never-halting time . . .

Michael's wife had two wheels, one for wool, one for flax; "if one had rest, it was because the other was at work." Her fire and her wheel were friends and comforters to the dame of the most solitary mountain cot, as was also

All day the house-clock ticking in mine ear.

The clock plays its part in Wordsworth's conception of the home. The Blea Tarn cottage had a solitary clock,

That on mine ear ticked with a mournful sound.

It is, says the poet, "an epoch, when the old house-clock is decked with a new face." The call of a cuckoo-clock pleased his own latter days.

Wordsworth's imagination delighted, again, in the cottage fare. Though he seems, owing perhaps in part to his defective sense of smell, to have had little appreciation of food,[1] he writes with enjoyment of the board spread with a napkin, "white as the foam of that rough brook by which it had been bleached," half covered with dainties,—oaten bread, curds, cheese, and cream; "a small parade of garden fruits;" whortle-berries from the mountain-side,

And cakes of butter curiously embossed,
Butter that had imbibed from meadow-flowers
A golden hue, delicate as their own
Faintly reflected in a lingering stream.

---

[1] "Mr. Wordsworth" "will live for a month on cold beef and the next on cold bacon." For "the Wordsworths never dine, you know; they hate such doings; when they are hungry they go to the cupboard and eat." Mary Russell Mitford thought to defame when, in one of her letters she wrote these words. This, however, is really the way the poetic should eat; no assembling for stodgy consumption three times a day, however genius or the weather may call, but
Seeking what he eats,
And pleased with what he gets.

Again, he writes of

Rich cream and snow-white eggs fresh from the
  nest,
With amber honey from the mountain's breast;
Strawberries from lane or woodland, offering
  wild
Of children's industry . . .

Or he describes the "cleanly supper-board," "with a
mess of pottage and skimmed milk," "oaten cakes and
plain home-made cheese."

It is the primitive nature of these foods, their nearness to the source whence they spring, their close relation to the labour of those whom they are to sustain
that makes them so interesting to Wordsworth, and so
worthy of his notice. Townsfolk, for whom water is
the cold or hot product of a pipe; whose food seemingly originates with the grocer and baker, or still more
artificially, in a restaurant, miss the poetry inherent in
these prime necessities as received directly from the
hands of Nature. It is unfortunately true that the
greater number of those whose lot gives them the opportunity to enjoy this poetry in the common round of
their daily life, also miss it, from native insensibility, or
from the deadening effect of excessive physical labour.
But in the Dalesmen of his time Wordsworth found the
capacity for something at least of this enjoyment.

The sense and love of home and land in these cottage
dwellers the poet saw as part of the love of Nature.

These simple folk would hardly have understood Nature or the love of it as an idea; but in fact their clinging to home and native spot was inseparable from the love of the vales and mountains, trees and fields, among which they had been born. The homesick dream of Poor Susan showed her a "mountain ascending, a vision of trees," "bright volumes of vapour," a river, "green pastures,"

> And a single small cottage, a nest like a dove's,
> The one only dwelling on earth that she loves.

In *Michael,* Wordsworth supremely shows how the life of the man was bound up in his land, his home; not *any* land or *any* home, but that particular mountain spot, his own, where he had been born and had lived for more than eighty years:

> And grossly that man errs, who should suppose
> That the green valleys, and the streams and rocks,
> Were things' indifferent to the shepherd's
>   thoughts.
> Fields, where with cheerful spirits he had
>   breathed
> The common air; hills, which with vigorous step
> He had so often climbed; which had impressed
> So many incidents upon his mind
> Of hardship, skill or courage, joy or fear;
> Which, like a book, preserved the memory
> Of the dumb animals, whom he had saved,
> Had fed or sheltered, linking to such acts
> The certainty of honourable gain;

Those fields, those hills—what could they less?
  had laid
Strong hold on his affections, were to him
A pleasurable feeling of blind love,
The pleasure which there is in life itself.

The land he feared to lose "looks as if it never could
endure another master."

"The degree and kind of attachment," writes the
poet in one of his notes, "which many of the yeomanry
feel to their small inheritances can scarcely be over-
rated. Near the house of one of them stands a magnificent tree, which a neighbour of the owner advised him
to fell for profit's sake. 'Fell it!' exclaimed the yeo-
man. 'I had rather fall on my knees and worship it.'"

The dalesfolk who "with covetous spirit" had sold
their fields were never again at peace—

We could do what we liked with the land, it was
  ours;
And for us the brook murmured that ran by its
  side . . .

But now,

I look at the fields, but I cannot go in—

"our birth-right was lost"—.

House, as well as land, is the centre of clinging
affections.

Wordsworth himself knew the deep longing for home
when away—

> O sad it is, in sight of foreign shores,
> Daily to think on old familiar doors,
> Hearths loved in childhood, and ancestral floors.

It is with a home that he would reward the "Louisa"
who won his approval by her passion, reproached by
others, for "long walks in the country." "She loves her
fire, her cottage-home," but will roam the moorland in
"weather rough or bleak;" a disposition which not only
wins the poet's affection, but makes the cottage-home
and fireside still more dear. She is promised a reward,—her own "nest in a green vale, a harbour and a
hold." Thus we return to the poet's ideal home—the
sheltered spot in Nature's midst, a refuge and place of
peace. In a phrase used elsewhere,

> The little Vale, a dwelling-place of Man,

the two thoughts, of seclusion and home, come at once,
as belonging to each other. There is another perfect
Wordsworthian home-site in the Lines to M. H. In
Rydal Upper Park is a slip of lawn and a woodland
pool,

> nor did sun
> Or wind from any quarter ever come
> But as a blessing to this calm recess,

227

This glade of water and this one green field.
The spot was made by Nature for herself . . .

This it is that makes a home, the daily association
with the beautiful, wild, or sublime works of Nature.
No matter how poor the dwelling, such association
makes it rich for feeling and memory. Spring works
her miracle, and

>   lowly huts, near beaten ways,
> No sooner stand attired
> In thy fresh wreaths, than they for praise
> Peep forth, and are admired.

The meanest, smokiest Highland hut takes on beauty
from Nature's hand:—

> See what gay wild flowers deck this earth-built
>   Cot
> Whose smoke, forth-issuing whence and how it
>   may,
> Shines in the greeting of the sun's first ray
> Like wreaths of vapour without stain or blot,
> The limpid mountain rill avoids it not;
> And why shouldst thou? . . .
> "Love, as Nature loves, the lowly Poor."

The home that for Wordsworth is thus in various
ways rooted in Nature, and dependent for its comfort
and charm on her, is also the creation of man, and is

again closely bound up with the human lot. Such ancestral, long-used dwellings are a sort of outer body of man, less sentient, slower in responding to the changes of his life, but still part of his being, moulded by his spirit, flourishing with his welfare, and falling away with his decay. The story of Margaret's ruined cottage is Wordsworth's great example of this truth. In the day of prosperity it was a cheerful object. The husband plied his busy spade after his daily work, till darkness hid every leaf and flower; and

> his careful hand
> At the first nipping of October frost,
> Closed up each chink, and with fresh bands of straw
> Chequered the green-grown thatch.

The garden had its treasures, as

> carnations,
> Prized for surpassing beauty, and no less
> For the peculiar pains they had required.

Sad reverses came upon the little household, and in the cottage and its surroundings we trace a gradual fall, as the Wanderer who tells the tale repeats his infrequent visits. At the first of these the cottage wore

> Its customary look—only, it seemed,
> The honeysuckle, crowding round the porch,
> Hung down in heavier tufts; and that bright weed,

The yellow stonecrop, suffered to take root
Along the window's edge, profusely grew,
Blinding the lower panes.

The garden lagged behind the season: the

daisy-flowers and thrift
Had broken their trim border-lines, and straggled
O'er paths they used to deck; carnations . . .
Declined their languid heads, wanting support.
The cumbrous bind-weed, with its wreaths and
bells,
Had wound about her two small rows of peas,
And dragged them to the earth.

The spot "though fair, was very desolate—the longer
I remained, more desolate." The corner-stones on either
side the porch were discoloured and stuck over with
tufts and hairs of wool, as if the sheep from the common came familiarly and "found a couching-place even
at her threshold."
At the next return,

her home
Bespoke a sleepy hand of negligence;
The floor was neither dry nor neat, the hearth
Was comfortless . . .

Her few books lay scattered, open or shut as they had
fallen. In the garden

weeds defaced
The hardened soil, and knots of withered grass;
No ridges there appeared of clear black mould,
No winter greenness; of her herbs and flowers,

> It seemed the better part was gnawed away
> Or trampled into earth; a chain of straw,
> Which had been twined about the slender stem
> Of a young apple-tree, lay at its root;
> The bark was nibbled by the truant sheep.

At the next visit the hut, no longer weather-fended, was sinking to decay, sapped by frost and thaw and rain. While Margaret slept,

>   The nightly damps
> Did chill her breast; and in the stormy day
> Her tattered clothes were ruffled by the wind,
> Even at the side of her own fire.

The plot of garden ground ran wild,

>   its matted weeds
> Marked with the steps of those whom, as they
>   passed,
> The gooseberry trees that shot in long lank slips,
> Or currants, hanging from their leafless stems,
> In scanty strings, had tempted to o'er leap
> The broken wall.

The well, in a "cold damp nook," was shrouded with willow-flowers and plumy fern;" a cheerless spot, a moss-grown useless fragment of a wooden bowl lying on its "slimy foot-stone."

We die, says the Wanderer, summing up the tale,

Not we alone, but that which each man loved
And prized in his peculiar nook of earth
Dies with him, or is changed . . .
                Beside yon spring I stood,
And eyed its waters, till we seemed to feel
One sadness, they and I. For them a bond
Of brotherhood is broken: time has been
When, every day, the touch of human hand
Dislodged the natural sleep that binds them up
In mortal stillness; and they ministered
To human comfort.

Thus to Wordsworth the home stood between man and Nature, a connecting bond; to temper her roughness, and partake of her sweetness; to be an expression of his life and character. So many illustrations have been given of this idea in its varying aspects, that it is clear why the cottage-home was so dear to him. How strong was his affection and peculiar feeling may be finally best summed up in some lines from the fifth of the *Poems on the Naming of Places,* describing that fair spot in Rydal Upper Park, with "its glade of water" and "one green field:"

The spot was made by Nature for herself;
The travellers know it not . . .
And if a man should plant his cottage near,
Should sleep beneath the shelter of its trees,
And blend its waters with his daily meal,
He would so love it, that in his death-hour
The image would survive among his thoughts.

Cole Orton Hall, Seat of Sir George Beaumount, Showing the Terrace and Rosary

II

The cottage, however, though always the dearest, was not the only manner of dwelling which interested Wordsworth. The larger country-house, or mansion, might share that peculiar charm of home if rightly planned and set in its surroundings. He would have "the fair front of many a happy home" made, or kept, a part of Nature. But in contrast to the cottage, which was so often naturally and originally in harmony with all about it, the larger house was likely to need design and care to bring it into perfect accord with its setting. An art is involved, the art of the landscape architect, in Wordsworth's day still called the landscape gardener.

For this art the poet believed himself to have a special calling, as well as for poetry, and for the criticism of pictures and works of art; and it is interesting to discover all that can be made out of his principles and practice.

He was no dabbler or trifler, but took the matter most seriously. Laying out grounds, he says in a letter to Sir George Beaumont on this subject, is a liberal art, whose object is to "assist Nature in moving the affections;" the affections, he explains, of those who have the "deepest perception of the beauty of nature," and thus "the most valuable feelings, that is, the most independent, the most ennobling, connected with Na-

233

ture and human life." And while all liberal arts should
make their appeal to enlightened minds, this must
above all be so

> when we are in the midst of the realities of
> things; of the beauty and harmony, of the joy
> and happiness of living creatures; of men and
> children, of birds and beasts, of hills and streams,
> and trees and flowers; with the changes of night
> and day, evening and morning, summer and win-
> ter; and all their unwearied actions and energies,
> as benign in the spirit that animates them as they
> are beautiful and grand in that form and clothing
> which is given to them for the delight of our
> senses!

The same strength of feeling inspires another passage
of this letter:

> I know nothing which to me would be so pleasing
> or affecting, as to be able to say when I am in the
> midst of a large estate—This man is not the vic-
> tim of his condition; he is not the spoiled child of
> worldly grandeur; the thought of himself does
> not take the lead in his enjoyments; he is, where
> he ought to be, lowly-minded, and has human
> feelings; he has a true relish of simplicity, and
> therefore stands the best chance of being hap-
> py . . .

The owner of the ideal estate is exhorted to

> do his utmost to be surrounded with tenants liv-
> ing comfortably, which will bring always with it
> the best of all graces which a country can have—

flourishing fields and happy-looking houses; and, in that part of his estate devoted to park and pleasure-ground, let him keep himself as much out of sight as possible; let Nature be all in all, taking care that everything done by man shall be in the way of being adopted by her.

It is important to note how Wordsworth thus bases the landscape art on human happiness and welfare, as well as on conformity with Nature. Probably the picturesque but comfortless hovel would have pleased him no more than such an excrescence on natural beauty as the tasteless boathouse built by a neighbour on the shore of Grasmere—"the utter detestation" of the poet and his household.

What should be the appearance of a house in a mountainous country Wordsworth had thoughtfully considered before he wrote his *Guide to the Lakes,* in which some of his views are set forth. He found most new buildings there too conspicuous, owing to the affectation of newcomers into the district, conscious that each new building would be looked at and commented on; owing, also, to the "craving for prospect . . . which is immoderate, particularly in new settlers;" so that houses "rise from the summits of naked hills in staring contrast to the snugness and privacy of the ancient houses."

Though in sympathy with the "desire to decorate . . . residence and possessions," his rule for it is simple; "with respect to grounds, work, where you can, in the spirit of Nature, with an invisible hand of art, Planting, and a removal of wood, may thus, and thus only, be carried on with good effect; and the like may be said of building, "if Antiquity, who may be styled the co-partner and sister of Nature, be not denied the respect to which she is entitled." He wishes the beautiful ancient forms of building, harmonising so happily with the forms of Nature, to be taken as models, "modern internal convenience" to be housed within their grace and dignity. If for reasons of expense or the like, this plan is not practicable, he would have the house in a mountainous country at least "not obvious, not obtrusive but retired."

For this rule he gives three good reasons. First, these regions with their reminders of the power of the elements, winds, snows, and torrents, "make the notion of exposure very unpleasing; while shelter and comfort are in proportion necessary and acceptable." Second, "Far-winding valleys difficult of access, and the feelings of simplicity habitually connected with mountain retirements, prompt us to turn from ostentation there as a thing eminently unnatural and out of place." And third, "a house in such scenes can never have sufficient dignity or interest to become principal in the landscape, and to render the mountains, lakes and torrents by which it may be surrounded, a subordinate part of the view."

The principle to which he leads us is that the house should be of such a size and so placed and constructed as to be "gently incorporated into the scenery of Nature." The same principle "should also determine its colour." "This rule should never be lost sight of—the colour of the house ought, if possible, to have a cast or shade of the colour of the soil." The house must harmonise with the surrounding landscape, and in mountainous countries especially, the rocks and parts of mountains where soil is visible should suggest the right colouring. Wordsworth points out, however, that this rule cannot be implicitly followed where the soil is "glaring red," or "sullen black," or the rocks have a blue tinge. A warm tint, he concludes, should be used, which, happily selected, does not disturb, but animates the landscape, as in the native cottages, where glaring whitewash has been subdued by time and weatherstains. And he recommends as safest "something between a cream and a dust-colour," condemning, as we have seen before (see page 151), white in buildings, for its obtrusiveness.

Wordsworth was not fanatical in his tastes, for even this quality of obtrusiveness, so decried by him, he is prepared to accept under fitting conditions.

> I like splendid mansions in their proper places, and have no objection to large, or even obtrusive, houses in themselves. My dislike is to that system of gardening which, because a house happens

to be large, or splendid, and stands at the head of a large domain, establishes it, therefore, as a principle that the house ought to *dye* all the surrounding country with a strength of colouring, and to an extent proportionate to its own importance. This system is founded, I think, in false taste—false feeling; and its effects are disgusting in the highest degree.

This domineering of the house over its country-side is one violation of the poet's principle that "the house should be so formed, and of such apparent size and colour, as to admit of its being gently incorporated with the works of Nature." The same principle, he believed should be applied to grounds and plantations; indeed, he thought it here even more urgent. Another violation, in respect to these, he criticises at the place of Price at Foxley, in Wales. This was comparatively small, yet

the domain is too extensive for the character of the country. Wanting both rock and water, it necessarily wants variety; and in a district of this kind, the portion of a gentleman's estate which he keeps exclusively to himself, and which he devotes, wholly or in part, to ornament, may very easily exceed the proper bounds—not, indeed, as to the preservation of wood, but most easily as to everything else.

238

"THE HAPPIEST-LOOKING HOMES OF MEN"

The power to control the forms of scenery becomes the law, he continues; the owner banishes all that does not please every mood, and from every point of view, thus "impoverishing and *monotonizing* landscapes, which if not originally distinguished by the bounty of nature, must be ill able to spare the inspiriting varieties which art, and the occupations and wants of life in a country left more to itself, never fail to produce." This "relish of humanity" Foxley wanted, and it was to him a melancholy spot.

In the *Guide to the Lakes* Wordsworth has much to say on the subject of planting. He is eloquent on the spoiling of natural beauties by mistaken practice, especially the indiscriminate planting of the larch, common at that time and place. But his general principles of planting are worthy of the attention of all interested in such matters, not only for their excellence, but as expounding truth with a poet's ardour and insight.

This teaching may be summed up in those two golden rules, impossible to emphasise too strongly: *let the images of Nature be your guide;* and *let there be an invisible hand of art working everywhere in the spirit of Nature.*

He points out that it is "not the removals, but the harsh *additions* that are made, which are always the worst grievance."

If no positive deformity or discordance be substituted or superinduced, such is the benignity of

Nature, that, take away from her beauty after beauty, and ornament after ornament, her appearance cannot be marred—the scars, if any be left, will gradually disappear before a healing spirit; and what remains will still be soothing and pleasing.

But—

what shall we say to whole acres of artificial shrubbery and exotic trees among rocks and dashing torrents, with their own wild woods in sight— when we have the whole contents of the nurseryman's catalogue jumbled together—colour at war with colour, and form with form?—among the most peaceful subjects of Nature's kingdom, everywhere discord, distraction, and bewilderment.

He entreats those who have a "lively feeling of the native beauty of these scenes" to

inquire of themselves wherein that beauty which they admire consists. They would then see that after the feeling has been gratified that prompts us to gather round our dwelling a few flowers and shrubs, which from the circumstances of their not being native, may, by their very looks, remind us that they owe their existence to our hands, and their prosperity to our care; they will see, that after this natural desire has been provided for, the course of all beyond has been predetermined by the spirit of the place.

Exotic plants thus should be "confined almost to the doors of the house;" but "a transition should be contrived, without abruptness, from these foreigners to the rest of the shrubs, which ought to be of the kinds scattered by Nature through the woods," or others carefully selected to harmonise with them, "especially with reference to colour, when the tints are most diversified, as in autumn and spring." Fruit-trees, both orchard and wild, "may be happily admitted as an intermediate link between the shrubs and the forest trees; which last ought almost.entirely to be such as are natives of the country."[1]

Wordsworth writes with a poet's feeling of the planting of woods, and of their proper beauties. "What endless melting and playing into each other of forms and colours" in the "hill overgrown with self-planted wood —each tree springing up in the situation best suited to its kind, and with that shape which the situation constrained or suffered it to take!"

He sets forth in detail the natural process of formation of woods and forests in the mountains. Seeds are scattered by winds, waters, or birds, and grow if, or as, the conditions allow. "From low and sheltered places vegetation travels upward to the more exposed, and

---

[1] In a letter to Beaumont the poet says: "I should not be for planting many forest trees about the house by the side of those which are already of their full growth. When I planted at all there, I should rather choose thickets of underwood, hazels, wild roses, honeysuckles, hollies, thorns, and trailing plants such as travellers' joy, etc. My reason, in addition to the beauties of these, is that they would never be compared with the grown-up trees, whereas young trees of the same kind will, and must appear insignificant."

the young plants are protected, and to a certain degree fashioned, by those that have preceded them." Their mass is broken by rocks, or open glades where animals have browsed. "As vegetation ascends, the winds begin also to bear their part in moulding the forms of the trees; but, thus mutually protected, trees, though not of the hardiest kind, are enabled to climb high up the mountains." Gradually, however, soil and exposure stop their ascent:

> the hardy trees only are left; those also, by little and little, give way—and a wild and irregular boundary is established, graceful in its feeling, more or less distinct, of the powers of Nature by which it is imposed.

He contrasts "the liberty that encourages, and the law that limits, this joint work of Nature and time," with the disadvantages under which the artificial planter must work, whose trees, even if well chosen, must generally start all at one time,

> and this necessity would of itself prevent that fine connexion of parts, that sympathy and organization ... which pervades the whole of a natural wood, and appears to the eye in its single trees, its masses of foliage, and their various colours, when they are held up to view on the side of a mountain; or when, spread over a valley, they are looked down upon from an eminence.

But, in planting

> let the images of Nature be your guide, and the
> whole secret lurks in a few words; thickets or
> underwoods—single trees—trees clustered or in
> groups—groves—unbroken woods, but with v.i.
> ied masses of foliage—glades—invisible or wind-
> ing boundaries—in rocky districts, a seemly pro-
> portion of rock left wholly bare, and other parts
> half hidden—disagreeable objects concealed, and
> formal lines broken—trees climbing up to the
> horizon, and in some places, ascending from its
> sharp edge, in which they are rooted, with the
> whole body of the tree appearing to stand in the
> clear sky—in other parts, woods surmounted by
> rocks utterly bare and naked, which add to the
> sense of height, as if vegetation could not thither
> be carried, and impress a feeling of duration,
> power of resistance, and security from change!

He who had thus learned the notes from which so
many harmonies of natural beauty are won was not
likely to go astray as a landscape gardener.

A characteristic beauty of the Lake District as
Wordsworth knew it, almost as lovely as its mountain
woods, was its network of "innumerable lanes and
pathways," "fenced by stone walls," and "mostly bor-
dered with ashes, hazels, wild roses, and beds of tall
fern at their base; while the walls themselves, if old,
are overspread with mosses, small ferns, wild strawber-

ries, the geranium, and lichens: and, if the wall happen to rest against a bank of earth, it is sometimes almost wholly concealed by a rich facing of stone-fern." The charm of these walls appealed to the landscape-gardener ı our poet, and his own garden-wall at Dove Cottage, backed by a bank of earth, was accordingly "exquisitely decorated with ivy, flowers, moss, and ferns, such as grow of themselves in like places." Though "a respectable person," one of the poet's neighbors, remarked that if *he* had to do with the garden, he would sweep away all the black and dirty stuff from the wall, yet present-day planters and gardeners may find Wordsworth's example full of suggestion. They may again be fired to imitation by the poet's poetic description of a forest path where he had paced many an hour with some of those he loved best:

> This path winds on under the trees with the wantonness of a river or a living creature, and even if I may say so with the subtlety of a spirit, contracting or enlarging itself, visible or invisible as it likes. There is a narrow slip of green turf besprinkled with flowers, chiefly daisies, and here it is, if I may use the same kind of language, that this pretty path plays its pranks, wearing away the turf and flowers at its pleasure.

Like the landscape painters, Wordsworth enjoyed animals in his scenery, and speaks with appreciation of the interest lent by the presence of cattle and sheep. After landing at Dover he wrote of the

> majestic herds of cattle, free
> To ruminate,

and observed that "this is a most grateful sight to an Englishman returning to his native land. Everywhere one misses in the cultivated grounds abroad, the animated and soothing accompaniment of animals ranging and selecting their own food at will."

Perhaps it was likewise a painter's instinct that lay behind his strong appreciation of bounded views, such as are naturally found in his native valleys, where the height of the mountains ensures "the aerial effects of distance . . . found even in the narrowest vales, where they lengthen in perspective or act . . . as telescopes for the open country." In his poems, several scenes that he presents for his own delight and ours are framed in various ways.[1] It will suffice here to notice the pleasant imagination, in one of the *Inscriptions* (on the island of Grasmere), of the shepherd who, when he looks from his bed through the open door-place toward the lake, wants not

> Creations lovely as the work of sleep—
> Fair sights, and visions of romantic joy!

---

[1] See *Light and Colour*, page 178.

A letter of Ellis Yarnall (who visited Rydal Mount) to Professor Henry Reed of Philadelphia describes a landscape artist's effect of the same sort, in the framed view of the lower waterfall at Rydal, seen from a summer-house in the grounds of Lady Fleming. The poet showed this to his guest, and "seemed to have much pleasure in exhibiting this beautiful retreat."

> The moment we opened the door, the waterfall was before us; the summer-house being so placed as to occupy the exact spot from which it was to be seen; the rocks and shrubbery around closing it in on every side. The effect was magical. The view from the rustic house, the rocky basin into which the water fell, and the deep shade in which the whole was enveloped, made it a lovely scene.

Wordsworth's pleasure in this legitimate piece of art is in strong contrast to his indignant *Effusion* on the "fantastic and uneasy" arrangements, in a pleasure-garden near Dunkeld, for viewing the cascade of the Bran, in innumerable mirrors on walls and ceiling.

Though he liked a framing of scenery in the spirit of Nature, Woodsworth did not approve of formal boundaries to grounds or portions of grounds. "Invisible, or winding boundaries," he demands; and a poem on Lady Beaumont's flower-garden makes a great point of its "viewless fence"—

> where the guardian fence is wound
> So subtly are our eyes beguiled
> We see not nor suspect a bound,—

and this "delicate Enclosure" seems to him an emblem of "modest kindness, that would hide the firm protection it bestows."

All that the poet says of gardens is most admirable. Thus:

> There are certain principles as to flower-gardens upon which my mind is made up . . . whenever a house fronts a grand or sublime scene of mountains, I would not admit beds of flowers and shrubs, with lawns interspersed . . . I would either have no flowers, or an architectural garden with terraces and formal beds, after the manner of the French or Italians.

And he continues, that "something of an antique air" is required in the house to suit this arrangement. If properly managed, the garden would be at once referred to the house and belong to it. In such places, he observes, "a disposition of flowers and shrubs and lawns which is neither Art nor Nature" is often seen, "to me displeasing to look upon."

When the landscape has no grandeur, but is of an "Arcadian character," "a little Cyclades of exotic shrubs and flowers may be introduced in front of a house with good effect."

As to the use of shrubs, Wordsworth lays down the rule now accepted by the mere beginner in laying out grounds:

> A wilderness of shrubs is a delightful thing as

part of a garden, but only as a part. You must have open space of lawn, or you lose all the beauty of outline in the different tufts or islands of shrubs, and even . . . in their individual forms.

Yes, he must have a lawn, to be

> a carpet all alive
> With shadows flung from leaves—to strive
> In dance, amid a press
> Of sunshine . . .

Before leaving the subject of flowers, it is worth while to note that Wordsworth had an eye for the beautiful and decorative in some of the humbler plants. "He must have a poor eye for beauty," he says, "who has not observed how much of it there is in the form and colour which cabbages and plants of that genus exhibit in the various stages of their growth and decay." (The poet would no doubt have sympathised with Andrew Fairservice's opinion, that "a kail-blaid or a colliflour glances so glegly by moonlight, it's like a leddy in her diamonds"). Again,

> A richer display of colour in vegetable nature can scarcely be conceived than Coleridge, my sister, and I saw in a bed of potato-plants in blossom . . . upon the moor between Inversneyd and Loch Katrine. These blossoms were of such extraordinary beauty and richness that no one would have passed them without notice. But the sense

must be cultivated through the mind before we can perceive these inexhaustible treasures of Nature, for such they really are.

No survey of Wordsworth's ideas of landscape-gardening can be complete without emphasising his sense of the supreme importance of light and shade. As in nature, so in the working of the "invisible hand of art," the play of sunshine and shadow, contrasts, harmonies, happy gradation of tones, aerial effects of distance, the changes of light and shade by hour and by season—all these must be reckoned and dealt with as the artist's most valuable possibilities. Since examples of Wordsworth's interest in these effects have been very freely given elsewhere in this book, it is not necessary to dwell further on them here. It is enlightening, however, to compare his taste in them with that of his contemporary Repton.

This admirable professional landscape-gardener in his book on the practice of the art observes:

> Certain objects appear best with the sun behind them, and others with the sun full upon them; and it is rather singular that to the former belong. all natural objects, such as woods, trees, lawn, water, and distant mountains, while to the latter belong all artificial objects, such as houses, bridges, roads, arable fields, and distant towns and villages.

Again, "Lawn, wood and water are always seen to the greatest advantage with the sun behind them, because the full glare of the light between opposite trees destroys the contrast of wood and lawn." He contrasts morning and evening views of the Thames (looking east) from Purley. In the morning "the wood was in a solemn repose of shade . . . dark hues were strongly contrasted by the vivid green of the meadows and the outline of distant hills was distinctly marked by the clearness of the atmosphere. I could scarcely distinguish any other object, but these formed a pleasing landscape, from the breath or contrast of light and shade." In the evening, "dark clouds reflected in the water made it almost invisible, the . . . wood presented one glare of rich foliage, not so beautiful in the painter's eye as when the top of each tree was relieved by small catching lights."

All this is at total variance with the ideas of Wordsworth, who in his *Guide* enjoins on the visitor the arrangement of his comings and goings so as to have the sun behind him in the vales. In a wood with the declining sun shining full upon it, Repton saw but a "glare" of rich foliage. Apparently he was regardless of the exquisite details of colour, of texture, of interwoven light and shadow in such an aspect, not to speak of the infinite varieties of form thus revealed. His eye, it would seem, craved mass, silhouette, and strong, broad and rich contrast, but missed the immense range of subtle and more delicate effects which Wordsworth sought. The poet's delight in these, however, meant no faint appreciation of the others; no one more loved tree masses against a sunset sky.

Wordsworth not only gave much thought to the principles of planting, he was ardent in practice, so far as his opportunities allowed. This is an interesting point in his character. Because in his private life his ways were sometimes not endearing, it is gratifying to find him in this matter so human, so eager, and brought so close by the tie that binds all who wield mattock or trowel.

At Dove Cottage William and Dorothy beautified their tiny precincts by planting many things, chiefly the native flowers, ferns, and mosses. Dorothy mentions white and yellow lilies, London Pride, periwinkle, lemon thyme, wild thyme, wild columbine, privet, orchises, lichens, mosses, snow-drops, gowans. Her brother wrote with delight of the snowdrops planted round a stone in the little orchard.

At Rydal he had more scope for his activities. A Windermere clergyman remarked "the surprising variety of natural beauties he managed to display to their best advantage, from the very circumscribed limits of the garden at Rydal Mount," and "how many there were who have owed the charm of their grounds and gardens to direction sought from his well-known taste and feeling."

FOUR STUDIES IN WORDSWORTH

John Taylor Coleridge (nephew of S. T. Coleridge) writes of Wordsworth:

> He combined, beyond any man with whom I ever met, the most unsophisticated poetic delight in the beauties of nature with a somewhat artistic skill in developing the sources and conditions of them. In examining the parts of a landscape he would be minute; and he dealt with shrubs, flower-beds, and lawns with the readiness of a practised landscape-gardener. His own little grounds afforded a beautiful specimen of his skill in this latter respect; and it was curious to see how he had imparted the same faculty in some measure to his gardener, James Dixon, I think, was his name.[1]

Rydal Mount under Wordsworth's care became a residence well suited to both poet and landscape-gardener. The house, facing south, stands on the sloping side of the rocky hill, Nab's Scar; a "modest mansion, of sober hue, tinged with weather stains;" a long two-storeyed dwelling, "mantled over here and there with roses and ivy, and jessamine and Virginia creeper." Besides its charm of lawn and garden, with trees and shrubs, its "beautiful glade, overhung with rhodendrons," its tall ash-tree, where the thrush sang for hours together, the special interest of the little

---

[1] For an amusing discussion between the poet and this gardener as to the condition of the lawn, see *Memoir of Wordsworth,* chap. 21.

place seems to have been its terraces, planned for the beauty of their views.

The first of these, the "upward sloping terrace," was reached from a gravel platform directly in front of the house by ascending to the westward "fourteen steps of stone about nine feet long, in the interstices of which grow the yellow flowering poppy and the wild geranium, or

> Poor Robin gay,
> With his red stalks upon a sunny day,

a favourite with the Poet, as his verses show." The sloping terrace reached by these steps was about two hundred and fifty feet long, shaded on the right by laburnums, Portugal laurels, mountain-ash and cherry trees, and flanked on the left by a "low stone wall, coped with rude slates, and covered with lichens, mosses, and wild flowers. The fern waves on the wall, and at its base grow the wild strawberry and fox-glove."

Beneath this wall was a "level terrace," a favourite resort of the poet in age, as easier for pacing. "Both these terraces command beautiful views of the vale of the Rothay, and the banks of the lake of Windermere." A path from the sloping terrace led at some distance to what the Wordsworth family called the "far terrace," on the mountain-side. This, "after wandering along in a serpentine line for about a hundred and fifty feet, ends at a little gate, beyond which is a beautiful well of clear water, called the Nab Well."

South of Wordsworth's kitchen-garden (not parted off from the other garden but "blended with it by parterres of flowers and shrubs"—the cabbages being deemed worthy of more refined neighbours) lay the bit of land called "Dora's Field," with a pool under an oak-tree, where the gold and silver fishes celebrated by the poet were placed for freedom. Wordsworth drained "a bit of spongy land" in this field, to make a "green terrace," comanding a beautiful view of the two lakes Rydal and Windermere, and more than two miles of intervening vale, with its stream.

But the poet's most interesting achievement in landscape-gardening was the winter-garden at Cole Orton, in Leicestershire. This, his most elaborate undertaking in this art, has an interest of the same sort as that which Browning found in Raphael's "century of sonnets," written with the silver pencil sacred to his drawwings, and in that picture of an angel which Dante meditated, to be outlined, perhaps, with the pen of the *Inferno*. Although here is no question of the romantic love which inspired the two great Italians, and led Browning, while citing, to imitate them, another passion, plainly to be felt, is at work,—that of the creative imagination. Certain chosen beauties, meanings, secrets of Nature and landscape are here swept, with a stir of the maker's being, into a design, a design which is to make its appeal through the eye.

This chief work in which Wordsworth "put to proof

art alien to the artist" he planned for Lady Beaumont, and in December, 1806, wrote her, as he says, the longest letter he had written in his whole life, describing the place as it was to be. Long the letter is, but so full of matter that it is difficult to summarise or abridge it. It, with Wordsworth's plan of the garden, is to be found in the *Letters of the Wordsworth Family* (now unfortunately out of print.)

The site of this garden was, in part, a small disused quarry, and thus it had the protection of a depressed situation. On this feature of the place the poet seized. He proposed to plant on top of the bounding and retaining walls a winding "line of evergreen shrubs mingled with cypress," and behind these "a row of firs, such as were likely to grow to the most majestic height." This planting he would continue around the garden (with a few openings to show two adjacent cottages) "so as to give it the greatest appearance of depth, shelter, and seclusion possible." "This is essential to the feeling of the place . . . of a spot which the winds cannot touch, which should present no image of chilliness, decay, or desolation," when these are everywhere else.

This idea of a protected, a halcyon spot, where life and growth go richly on, and outer bleakness and frost are forgotten, is worked out by the poet in full, careful, and fine details. The boundary, so essential to the existence of such an oasis, is planned not only to seclude and protect, but also for much variety of beauty.

The wall, with "recesses, buttresses, and towers" was to be covered here and there with ivy and pyracanthus, or "any other winter plants that bear scarlet berries and are rich and luxuriant in their leaves and manner of growing." A perpendicular bank was to be planted with "ivy, periwinkle, and other beautiful or brilliant evergreen trailing plants which should hang down and leave the earth visible in different places. From the *sides* of the bank also might start juniper or yew, and it might be sprinkled over with primroses." As for the remains of the little quarry, "I would scratch the bank here, so as to lay bare more of the sand rock, and that in as bold a way as could be done. This rock or *scar* . . . I would adorn with trailing plants, and juniper, box, and yew-tree, where a very scanty growth would soon show itself." Of an unsightly corner with an old ugly wall, he says, "Here I would plant, to cover this wall, a hedge of hollies, or some other evergreen, which should not be suffered to grow wildly, but be clipped, making a wall of verdure to ascend to the roots of the fir-trees that are to be planted upon the top of the bank." The formality of this would "revive the artificial character of the place in a pleasing way, preparing for a return to the new stone wall; the parts of the whole boundary thus . . . either melting into each other quietly, or forming spirited contrasts."

At the steps descending into the garden he proposes to diversify by bringing in water to "trickle down the

The Steps Leading Down into the Wordsworth Garden
The Wych Elm where the water was to be introduced is at the top of these

bank about the roots of the wych elm;" if not a waterfall, at least "a dripping of water," round which "vivid
masses" of water-plants might grow, which, "when
cased in ice, form one of the most enchanting appearances that are peculiar to winter." And, to crown the
charms of this boundary, the poet requests one opening, "but scarcely more, . . . which should present the
best view of the most interesting distant object."

Within its secluding walls and banks this winter retreat is to be furnished with a variety of delights. No
deciduous trees are to be admitted, as jarring with the
sentiment of the place. Its several "compartments,"
each in a different spirit, are to be alike in presenting
only the plants which are at their best in the season of
cold. A path following the boundary, but not always
showing it, is to wind about the place, leading from one
interest to another.

Beginning at the "old steps," it will follow the wall,
which as "the most artificial ought to be the most
splendid and ornamental part of the garden." Between
wall and walk here is to be a box-edged border, "to re-
ceive the earliest and latest flowers." Snowdrops and
crocuses are to be next the boxwood; close under the
wall a "row or fringe of white lilies, and in front of
this another of daffodils." The middle of the border is
to be "richly tufted or bedded over with hepatica, jon-
quils, hyacinths, polyanthuses, auriculas, mezereon, and
other spring-flowers, and shrubs that blossom early;

and for the autumn, Michaelmas daisy, winter-cherry, china-asters, Michaelmas and Christmas rose," and many others.

The wall, fronting south, is to have toward its eastern corner a glade below it, open to the sun and bounded east and west by "little long" hillocks formed of rubbish, planted with a line of evergreen shrubs extending south beyond them. The glade is to be broken by one or two "trees of the cypress kind, which would spire up without excluding the sun." This "first compartment" will be characterised by ornament of architecture, the wall, and also by "showiness or splendour of colour in the flowers (which should be chiefly garden flowers) and in the choice of the shrubs." Here if possible, was to be a stone fountain, the stone to be in accord with the wall; the sparkling water with the bright hues of the flowers.

Continuing our way towards the left, the second compartment is to be a glade unelaborate and simple, surrounded with evergreens with a few in the middle. A view of an ancient ivy-hung cottage is to be "the presiding image here." There will be no border, and only wild flowers, scattered everywhere.

Next comes a dark thicket or grove, with the path winding through as far as the second cottage. The path now crosses an outlet to the high-road, the door to this to be entirely concealed by a thick arch of evergreens. The next glade or "compartment" will be open, "belted round with evergreens, quite unvaried and secluded." Here is to be a basin of water with two gold or silver fish, the "genii" of the pool and place. The spot is to be as monotonous as possible in colour—"the enclosure of evergreens, the sky above, the green grass floor, and the two mute inhabitants, the only images it should present unless here and there a solitary wild-flower."

Next comes the little quarry, to be filled with a pool of water, to reflect rocks, hanging plants, the firs on top, and, "shooting deeper than all, the spire of the church." This recess, under a ridge of rubbish, is to be bare and grassy, planted only on top with tall-growing trees, to give as much depth as possible.

The path leads on, coming suddenly by a turn to the "new steps" under the clipped holly hedge, near the wych elm with its dripping water. A little farther are the "old steps," where our tour began. Between them and the first glade an alley is to start, running north and south through the garden. It is to be perfectly straight and level, shaded with evergreens; probably laurels, as growing fastest. The floor is to be green and mossy, when the trees overshadow, "so that the whole would be still, unvaried, and cloistral, soothing and not stirring the mind, or tempting it out of itself." The upper end is to be closed by evergreens, the southern by "a rising bank of green turf, to catch the light and present a cheerful image of sunshine, as it would always appear to do, whether the sun shone or not, to a person walking in the alley when the vista shall have become a complete shade."

Such are the outlines of the winter-garden, over the planning and partial executing of which the poet enormously enjoyed himself, as a letter of his sister's testifies.[1] The garden had other features, some of which its creator produced with his own hands. Besides making several "inscriptions" for various trees, urns, and seats in the Beaumont grounds, Wordsworth, with his wife and sister, while overseeing the workmen in the winter garden, amused himself by scooping a seat out of soft sandstone rock, "almost the size, with something of the appearance, of a stall in a Cathedral." There was also a cedar at Cole Orton "planted by Beaumont's and by Wordsworth's hands."

Not only did he enjoy planting as well as planning; he planted sometimes out of pure benevolence, for the fitness of things, and that others might benefit. Through his influence, under his own eye, and partly by his own hand, a number of yew-trees were planted in Grasmere church-yard, looking forward to a time when, by their growth

---

[1] It is to be regretted that this plan, so interesting in every detail, was never fully carried out. For example, there are deciduous trees with the firs and cedars which form the elevated boundary of the garden. There is no central walk from north to south, as Wordsworth planned; consequently, no grassy mound to catch the light, and give an effect of sunshine when there is none. And, though divided into "compartments" by screens of trees and shrubs, the garden is in parts much overgrown, so that it is difficult to get satisfying views; and Wordsworth's fine distinctions of course cannot exist.

"Scott's Seat" in the Wordsworth Garden; Apparently the One Hollowed out by the Poet and His Sister. (See p. 260)

a solemnity will be spread over the place that will in some degree make amends for the old simple character which has already been so much encroached upon, and will be still more every year.

He recommends to the Beaumonts the planting of holly:

For its own beauty, and for the sake of the hills and crags of the North, let it be scattered here in profusion [in the winter-garden]. It is of slow growth, no doubt, but not so slow as generally supposed, and somebody, we hope, will enjoy it.

Wordsworth particularly loved holly, and an account of his landscape and planting work may well end with a pleasant picture showing the survival in age (August, 1841, when he was seventy-one) of the interests of his youth. A neighbour at Rydal, Mrs. Fletcher, relates how, walking on the terrace with her,

he was struck with the berries on the holly tree, and said, "Why should not you and I go and pull some berries from the other side of the tree, which is not seen from the window? and then we can go and plant them in the rocky ground behind the house." We pulled the berries, and set forth with our tool. I made the holes, the Poet put in the berries. He was as earnest and eager about it as if it had been a matter of importance; and as he put the seed in, every now and then he muttered, in his low solemn tones, that beautiful verse from Burns's *Vision:*

261

And wear thou this, she solemn said,
And bound the holly round my head.
The polished leaves and berries red
    Did rustling play;
And like a passing thought she fled
    In light away.

He clambered to the highest rocks on the "Tom Intach," and put in the berries in such situations as Nature sometimes does with such true and beautiful effect. He said, "I like to do this for posterity. Some people are selfish enough to say, What has posterity done for me? but the past does much for us."

It is appropriate to leave Wordsworth enjoying this particular "homefelt pleasure;" for it *was* to him one of the essential pleasures of a home. Given a harbour and a hold, in the keeping of Nature, the duty and delight of the home-owner is to maintain those delicate relations, that Nature may still seem to be "all in all," and man indeed her child, not her invader and despoiler. Thus, "working in the spirit of Nature with an invisible hand of art," are formed those "happiest-looking homes of men," which shall not only awaken our sense of the beautiful and the fitting, but shall by their harmony, their foundation on deep, on vital feeling, actually raise and support the spirit of dweller and beholder.

APPENDIX: WORDSWORTH'S AND KEATS'S LIGHT AND COLOUR WORDS

The words of a poet, the physical material of his craft, have a strong attraction of their own. As for light and colour words, they are so irresistible that it has seemed worth while to make a list of those used by Wordsworth, in the hope that they may be of some general interest. It has been thought, too, that much might be suggested by a comparison with the vocabulary of another poet. Therefore Keats's light and colour words have also been listed; Keats being chosen because one naturally thinks of him as a colourist, and in this respect a contrast to Wordsworth.

Such vocabularies are of course quite unfair to the colour and light sense or expressions of either poet, since words torn from their context keep so little of their poetic value.[1] *Stains, blush'd* or *dyes* read in a list suggest something; but what are they to

> Innumerable of stains and splendid dyes
> As are the tiger-moth's deep damask'd wings . . .

or

> A shielded scutcheon blush'd with blood of
> queens and kings. . . . . . . ?

---

[1] Unfair, again, because though an idea expressed as a compound word is included, the same idea without the hyphen is not. Thus, *red-deer, dull-red;* but not *red deer, dull red.*

APPENDIX

One is often puzzled in making such a list. Do words such as *smoke, steam, frost-built, dreary, sunward, cloud-capped,* to mention only a few, stand sufficiently for effects of light or its absence to be included? Should words implying chiefly mere ideas of vision, like *far-descried, unseen, blind, distinguishable, veiled,* have a place? It has seemed best, when there was doubt, even strong doubt, to include rather than not; since by taking in the questionable words we at least get a better idea of how wide was Wordsworth's interest in the visible.

WORDSWORTH'S LIGHT AND COLOUR WORDS[1]

alabaster *albinos *amaranthine amber azure *bar (blue bar of solid cloud) beam beamed beaming *beamless *beamy *bedim *bedimmed *bedimming bedims bespangled black *black-blue *blackened blackening blackens *blacker *blackest *blackness *blanch blanched *blaze *blazed blazes blazing bleach blind (mountain's silent top) blinded *blinder (vacancy) *blindfold *blinding *blindly blindness *blink (stars begin to) blood *blood-drop *blood-drops *bloodless blood-red *blood-reeking blood-stained bloody bloom

---

[1] Words not used by Keats (in a light or colour sense) are marked with an asterisk. Merely *literal* variations, as *barr'd, barred, parti-coloured, party-coloured, blacke, black,* have not been noticed; but the different parts of verbs, and plurals and possessives of nouns are counted, as having distinct meaning.

APPENDIX

blooming *blooms blot *blots *blotted blush blushed
blushes blue *blue-breeched brazen bright brighten
brightening *brightens brighter brightest bright-eyed
bright-haired brightly brightness brilliant bronzed
brown *browner burn burned burning burns burnt
burnished *candle-light *carnation cerulean *chalky
checquered *checquering *checquerings cherry *clear-
blue clearer *clearest clearly clearness *clear-shining
*clear-sighted *clear-white cloud *cloud-capped
clouded cloudless *cloud-like *cloud-loving (hill)
clouds *cloud-sequestered (heights) *cloud-streaks
*cloud-wooing (hill) cloudy coal-black colour coloured
*colouring colours coral *crescent-moon *cresset
*cressets crimson *crimson-spotted crystal crystalline
*crystals dappled *dappling dark *dark-blue *dark-
brown darken darkened darkening *darkens *darker
darkest dark-eyed *dark-green darkling *darkly darkness *darksome dawn dawned dawning *dawn-light
*dawns day day's days *days' *daybreak *daylight
*day-spring *day-star dazzle dazzled *dazzles dazzling
deep-yellow (beams; deep quiet gloom) deepen'd
(darkness) deepening (soft gloom deepening) *deepens (evening deepens into night) deeper (than the
Tyrian dye; blue; shadows) deepest (purple; bronzed
with deepest radiance) *deeply (more deeply tinged)
depth (azure; depth of shade) diamond diamonds
*diaphanous dim *dim-discovered *dim-eyed *dim-

gleaming *dimmed *dimmer *dimmest *dimming dimness dim-seen *dim-twinkling distinct *distinctly distinctness distinguishable *distinguishes *distinguishing
drear *drearier *dreariest *dreariness dreary dull
*dullest *dull-red dusk dusky *dusky-browed *dusky-
white dye dyed *earth-sullying ebon eclipse *eclipsed
eclipsing *effulgence embers *embrowned emerald
empurpled *enlightened *ensanguined Erebus eve
eve's even evening *evening-moon evening's evenings
eventide *extinguish *extinguished fade faded fades
fading faint fainter faintest faintly *faints fallow-
deer[1] *far-beaming *far-descried *far-seen fierce
(orbs abate their glare) fiercest (sun) fiery film *filmy
fire *fire-clad *fireless *fire-like fires fireside *firesides
*fireworks flame *flame-eyed flames *flameward
flaming flaring flash flashed flashes *flashing
fleecy-white *florid (hues) flush flushed foam
*foam-balls foamed *foaming *foam-lit *foamy
fog *fresh *freshen *fresher *freshness frost
*frost-built *frosting *frost-like *frost's *frosts
frosty fulgent *full (moon) full-orbed Galaxy
*gauds gaudy gay *gayest gem *gemmed gems
*gem-like *ghastly *ghost-like (image of a cloud)
gild gilded *gilding gilds *gilt *glance *glances
glancing glare glares glaring glass *glassed
glassy *glazed (eye) *glead gleam *gleamed
gleaming gleams *gleamy glimmer glimmered

---

[1] Keats has "fallow stag."

glimmering glimpse glimpses *glinted glisten glistened glistening *glistenings glistens *glitter glittered glittering glitters gloom gloomier *gloomiest glooms gloomy glories *glorified *glorify glorious glory *gloss glow glowed glowing glows glow-worm *glow-worm's glow-worms gold golden *golden-haired gorgeous *grain-tinctured grass-green green *greener greenest *greenness *green-grown *green-leaved *greensward *green-tinged *greenwood grey grey-beard *grey-clad *grey-haired *grey-headed gules *half-extinguished *half-moon *half-seen *half-veiled *halo *harebell (eyes) haze hazel *hazy heaven heaven's heavens *heaven-lit *heavenly (bodies shining in their spheres) Hesperus *hill-shadow hoar *hoar-frost hoary *hoary-headed hue hues ice *ice-built icy illume *illuminate *illuminating *illumination *illumine *illumined *illumines image *imaged imagery images *imbue (the prison bars with solemn sheen) *imbued *imbues *indistinctly *inflamed *inter-lunar invisible invisibly Iris *irradiate *irradiation *jet jewel *joy-flushes Jove (planet) *keen[1] (as a frosty star) *keenly *kindle *kindling *kindlings lamp *lamp-lighter lamps *lantern (the gloomy lantern and the dim blue match) *lantern's *laurel-shaded *leaf-green light lighted

---

[1] Keats has the uncertain "silver bow and arrows keen" of the hunt-ress moon.

lightning *lightning's lightnings lights *limpid
*livelier *liveliest liveliness (a more than sunny
liveliness) *lively (the lively beauty of the
leopard) *living (hue) Lucifer *luminary *luminous *lunar *lurid lustre lustres *lymph *mantle
*many-tinted marble (neck) *Mars *mellow
(light; a freshening lustre mellow) *mellowing
mid-day mid-night *mild (splendour; moonlight
fascinations mild; three paly loopholes mild and
small) *milder *mildly (bright) *mildly-gleaming
milk-white *Milky Way mirror *mirror's mirrors mist
mists misty moon moonbeam moonbeams *moon-
illumined moonless moonlight *moonlight-loving
moonlight's *moonlit moon's moons moonshine
morn morning morning's mornings *morning-star
*mountain-shades *mountain-snows *mountain-sun-
beams murky *negress *negro *never-fading
*never-sullied night nightfall *nightfire night's
(ethereal blue; night's starless gloom) nights
*night-time noon (cheerful noon; glare of noon;
blaze of noon) noonday noontide obscure ob-
scured *obscurities *obscurity *o'ershade *o'er-
shadow *o'ershrouds *olive (green) orange orb
*orbs *Orion (constellation) *outshine *outshining
*overshade *paint *painted *painter painter's[1]
*paints (the checquered bow that paints the
sky) pale *pale-blue *pale-faced paleness paler

---

[1] Of the words in this group Keats has but one, used once: "heroic
tints that pain a painter's sense."

APPENDIX

*pale-visaged pallid *paly parti-coloured *pea-green pearl pearls pearly pearly-white Phoebus *pictured *pictures pink *pink-vested planet planetary (the planetary Five) planet's planets *Pleiads *poppy (adj.) pure *purer *purest *purity purple *purpled *purpling *purpureal *radiance *radiant rainbow *rainbow-arch *rainbow-coloured *rainbow's rainbows *raven's (in colour like a raven's wing) ray rays redbreast redbreasts *red-brown *red-cross *red-deer *redden reddened *reddening *red-haired red-hot *red-ribboned reflect reflected reflection reflections reflects *reflex (of a star) refract (in rainbow hues the restless fire) resplendent rich (golden verdure, rich and dazzling sheen) *richly (how richly glows the water's breast) *rime *rimy rose rosebud (adj.) roseate *roses rosy *rosy-cheeked *rubies ruby ruddy *russet *rusty sable *sable-blue *saffron *sallow sapphire scarlet *sea-green *self-illumined shadowed shadows shadowy shady *sheen shine shines shining shone silver *silver-bright *silver-collared silvered silvering *silver-rimmed silvery *Sirius skies sky *sky-built skyey *sky's *smiling (plot of green; sea; fair smiling lights the purpled hills illume) smoke *smokeless *smoke-wreath *smoking *smoky snow *snow-clad *snows snow-white snowy sober (colourings) *soil (lips coloured like the

soil) soiling *solemn (colouring of the night;
effulgence) sombre *sombrous sooty spangled
spark sparkle sparkles sparkling *sparklings
sparks speck *speckless *specks *spectral (lakes
bemocking thirsty men) splendid splendidly
splendour *splendour's *splendours spot spotless
spots spotted *spotting *stain stained *stainless
stains star *star-bright *star-crowned *starless
star-light *starlike starry stars *star-spotted
*steam (breathed a pale steam around the
glaring hills) *steaming (lake; rills) *steeled
(waters) *still-twinkling *stormy (fire) streak
streaked streaks Stygian sullen *sullenly (glaring) *sullied *sullies sully sun sunbeam *sunbeam's sunbeams *sun-bright sunburnt *sun-gilt
*sunless *sunlight *sun-like sunlit *sunniest sunny
*sun-proof sunrise sun's suns sunset sunshine
*sunshining *sunshiny *sunward *swanlike taper
*taper-light *taper-lights taper's tapers tawny
*tender (green) *three-striped (banner) *thun-
der-cloud *tincture (clouds of all) *tinctured
(daintily with florid hues) tinge tinged tints
*torch torches *translucent *transparence *trans-
parency transparent *turbid twilight *twilight's
*twinkle *twinkles *twinkling *twinklings *Tyrian
(dye) *unbedimmed *unblemished (moon) *un-
burnished undazzled undefiled undimmed *undis-
cerning (night) *undiscoloured *undyed *unen-

lightened (not sunless gloom or unenlightened) *unextinguished unfaded unfading *unillumined *unmellowed (light) unseen *unshaded *unstained unsullied *veil (of glory for the ascending moon) *veiled veins *Venus (planet) verdant verdure vermeil vermilion Vesper violet vivid *vividly *vividness wan *wane *waned *waning *weather-stains white *white-cliffed whitened whiteness *whitening *whitens whiter *white-rimmed *white-robed *white-sleeved whitest yellow *yellowed *yellowing.

KEATS' LIGHT AND COLOUR WORDS NOT USED BY WORDSWORTH

amaranth amber-fretted amethyst Apollo ardent (marigolds) argent auburne Aurorian (clouds) azure-lidded barred bars (frecklings, streaks, and bars) beacon beamily beaminess benighted blackamoor blackberries black-eyed black-weeded black-winged blear'd blear-eyed bloodshot bloom (vb.—barred clouds bloom the soft-dying day) bloomy blue-eyed bluely blushful blushing blushingly blush-tinted bright-blanch'd bright-mail'd bright-winged brilliance brilliances bronze chequer Cimmerian cinque-coloured clear-eyed cloudiness cloudlet cloudlet's cloudlets cloudlets' cream creamy crescent crescents crimsons Cynthia Cynthia's damask dapple dark-cluster'd dark-grey dark-leav'd dark-stemmed day-tide day-time death-pale death-shadows deep-damask'd deep-green deep-seen Dian Dian's distinctness drear-nighted dull-eyed dun dusking ebon-tipped ebony em-purple enshaded eves extinct (lamps) fadeth fadingly faint-lipped (shells) fair-hair'd fiercer (brilliances) filmed films fire-tail'd fire-wing'd flame's flare flared flash'd flickering flushing foggy forest-green freckled freckles freckle-wing'd frecklings frosted frost-white froth frothy gleam-ings glimmers gloam gloombird's gloriously gold-en-browed golden-feathered gold-finches gold-fish[1] gold-green gold-tinted green'd green-fan'd green-head green-hills greening green-kyrtled green-recessed green-rob'd greens green-weed grey-brow'd grey-gone grey-growing grey-grown greyly hectic hue-golden Hyperion icicles ice-drops illuminings impearl'd ink'd (purple) ivory ivory-headed jet-black jetty jewel'd jewelries jewel'ry jewels jewel-sceptres kindled lilly[2] (hand; shoulders) lilly-feminine Lincoln-green livid lucent lustrous mantling marbled meadow-green meteor-star mild-er-mooned milky mirror'd misting moonbeamy morning-bright motley mottled muddy o'erdark-ened o'ershadowing olive[3] (brow) orbing orby

---

[1] Wordsworth has, of course, two poems entitled *Gold and Silver Fishes.*
[2] Wordsworth has the suggestion of colour in "virgin lilies marshalled in bright row."
[3] Wordsworth's one olive is olive green.

APPENDIX

(power of moon) outblackens outsparkling over-
shadoweth overshadows over-spangled painter's
paled pale-mouth'd pearl-built pearl'd pearliest
pearl-pav'd Phoebe Phoebe's purely purple-lined
purple-stained purplish Queen-moon rainbow-sided
raven (horses) raven-sombre red-lin'd red-lipped
resplendently richness (deepening to richness
from a snowy gleam) rose-bloom rose-warm
rubiest rubious rubious-ardent sable-pointed san-
guineous sapphir'd sapphire-region'd sapphires
sapphire-warm sea-foamy semi-lucent semi-shaded
shading shadowings silver-clear silver-footed sil-
verly silver-proud silver-white silver-wing snow-
clouds snow-light soft-dying (day) spangler
spangles spangling spangly sparkled speckled
spectres (busy in a cold, cold gloom) splen-
dider Star-Queen's starr'd streaking sunbeamy
swart tann'd taper-flame thunder-gloomings tinging
tinsel tint tinted tinting Titian (Titian colour
touch'd into real life) torch's turquoise unveil'd
Uranus (starry) veiling vein vein'd verd'rous
vermilion-spotted vermilion-tail'd Vesper's viewless
wannish white-flower white-handed whitely white-
plumed.

APPENDIX

light		colour
295	words common to both poets	121
247	words peculiar to Wordsworth	131
126	words peculiar to Keats	135
542	Wordsworth's total	252
421	Keats's total	256

The *number of uses* of the words does not of course enter into this summary at all, nor does any account of the immensely different amount of work done by the two poets. Such a summary, again, must be defective, since it is impossible to separate light and colour feeling in certain words, such as *pearly, gold, silver, ghastly, blazing, fiery,* and even plain *black* and *white.* Each word has here been reckoned but once; but in these and other cases the distinction can be only arbitrary.

So much for the value of figures in such an estimate! But at least they, and the words themselves, show that Wordsworth's vocabulary, much richer (as one would expect) in light and shade than that of Keats, is also rather surprisingly strong in colour.